To Dal...
La...

Black Tracks

Black Tracks

NINETEEN YEARS ON THE MAINLINE

by

FLOYD MILES, JR.

as told to

Irene Burk Harrell

LOGOS INTERNATIONAL

Plainfield, New Jersey

Standard Book Number: 0-912106-29-8
Library of Congress Catalog Card Number: 77-161424
Logos, International
185 North Avenue
Plainfield, New Jersey 07060

Printed in the United States of America

Dedicated to these dead and living dead
with my prayer that it might
do God's glory some good
turning those who are suffering
a living death in the bondage of drugs and sin
to Him who is Life abundant and everlasting

° ° °

YOUNGBLOOD—walked out of the hospital and died.

SYCE—died in the hospital.

EDDIE—found dead in his room of an OD after three days.

CLEAN HEAD—killed down south, running from being killed by pushers in New York City.

SONNY—found dead in hallway in the Bronx from an overdose.

JOE, a neighbor who grew up with me—found on roof, dead from overdose.

RAY—killed, head split open by a fellow junkie.

HONEY BOY, Ray's brother—blew his mind and went to prison.

TOY, one of my girls—drank and doped herself to death.

SPUNGY BOY—still hangin' on.

SPUNGY GIRL—one of the first girls to die from an overdose.

JERRI—addict who drank herself to death.

KITTY—dead from drugs and liquor.

RED—died from an overdose after he was released from Rickers Island Jail.

BIG BOY—addict serving life in prison for homicide.

CHESTER—pusher who died in federal pen.

TEDDY, one of the greatest dancers—dead from an overdose.

JACK—addict who died from drugs and liquor at the age of twenty-five.

CALIFORNIA JIMMY—blew his mind; still walking the streets like he is out of this world.

DUKE—on drugs and liquor until he ruined his health and died with TB.

DANNY—pickpocket who died with an overdose, never in the street long enough to get a habit.

SWIFTY—gifted singer, boxer, and warm-hearted dude stabbed in a fight over drugs in a Fulton Street bar in Brooklyn. Buried in Potters' Field on Harts' Island.

RED EYE—died with an overdose.

SUNNY—beaten to death in a 126th Street bar in front of friends, fighting over drugs.

GEORGIA—died from drugs and goof balls.

POPEYE—still dwindling away.

FLASH—slowly being eaten up by wine and dope.

CONNIE—once beautiful, now wasting away.

SHIRLEY and JIMMY—years together in hell.

BUGS—still bound, can find no peace, no rest.

Spain, Moon, Turk, Danny, Youngblood, Country, Vivian, Slim, Scope, Steve, Edna, Russell, Nate, Irene, Roberta, Diane, Harold, Vince, Herbie, Dice, Bernard, Bummy Boy, Ronnie, Diamond, Rita, Horse, Slapo, Sam, Porgie, Dickie, Chicago Shorty, Chi, Genie . . . God knows the rest. The list never stops.

Chapter I

"Hey, you there—Miles!"

We were shuffling out of the weathered red work-house to go to the ballfield for recreation when the blue-uniformed guard yelled at me. The line of prisoners stopped in their tracks on the worn concrete side-walk outside the dorms at Harts' Island Prison in New York City. Everybody turned to look at me, the dull wooden faces showing sparks of life and the drooping shoulders lifting at the unexpected break in the day's dead routine.

What have I done now? I wondered. *I'm gittin' short—just two weeks to go. Oh, don't let nuthin' go wrong!*

The sudden quietness wrapped around me like a smothering blanket, and the strong disinfectant stink of the prison pushed its way into my nose and throat as I took a quick sharp breath.

The hack's face looked sad, somehow, like he was sorry about something. My eyes took in the rest of him —the stiff straight way he carried himself, the shiny buttons on his jacket, the sharp creases in his pants— while I waited. He pulled a wrinkled yellow paper from his pocket and thrust it toward me, keeping his eyes open, waiting to see how I'd react.

I'd never received a telegram before, but I'd seen them plenty of times. They generally meant bad news. I could feel my back tense up as my hands fumbled at unfolding the paper and smoothing out the creases.

"Naomi died in hospital yesterday," it said. "Funeral Tuesday. Your sister-in-law, Joyce."

I just stood there, trying to stir in my mind and see if I could believe it.

Naomi? Naomi dead? What from? She's so young! My wife gone forever? Somewhere outside a dog howled, like he was grieving for her, like maybe the telegram was true. I shook my head. It was no use. I couldn't believe it.

Oh, God, no! Naomi can't be dead! She hasn't started livin' yet! She's only twenty-five!

A thousand other "no's" shoved each other around inside my head. And I asked myself a million questions:

What'll happen to our kids? How come her? Why

not me? God is good?? No way in the hell I could think so, not just then.

I stood there, cussing Him under my breath until the line started moving again, like a row of tin soldiers pushing each other along. I moved with them, folding the telegram and sliding it between the buttons into the front of my shirt where it rested cool and crinkling against my skin.

"I'm sorry, Miles," the hack said as he herded us along toward the field. I nodded at him, not trusting my voice to speak. My throat couldn't swallow; my eyes burned like fire.

Going along like a robot in the line of men, I kept thinking about Nay and me, remembering the first time I ever saw her . . .

She was with my friend Turk at his apartment one day in the spring when I went to see him after his mother had gone to work. She was a neighborhood girl —I'd seen her around, but had never really noticed her before. That day she looked different, somehow, and I found myself staring at her. And she was looking back at me.

Turk noticed it right away, that there was some kind of magic happening between us, and he kind of joked about it.

"Hey, Bunky, no need to get excited about Naomi," he grinned, his smile showing a big black space where two front teeth had been knocked out in a fight; "she's just a baby next to you. Only fourteen—"

"Naomi, huh?" I said, ignoring the rest of it. Her

name felt good in my mouth. *Naomi.* She was a rich dark brown, warm and friendly looking. I could tell by the way she snapped her fingers and tapped her foot in time to the music coming in the window from the drugstore piccolo, a jukebox on the corner, that she must like to dance. Her eyes were dancing already, sparkling, full-of-fun eyes. They made me want to drown in them.

It was hard to believe she was only fourteen. Already she had curves in all the right places, and she acted like she knew the score.

"She use dope?" I asked Turk later, nodding my head in Naomi's direction when the three of us were walking to the candy store and she stopped to speak to a friend.

"Naw, man," he said. "She don't use—she just turnin' *me* on, getting scratch for my habit."

I smiled, being glad she wasn't an addict, and I made a date with her, to go up to her place that night after the flick. Naomi was my girl from that day on. Eleven years . . .

Walking through the dusty prison yard, I shivered, but not from the breeze that rattled the dry leaves in the fence corners and kicked the dust up in my face. My shivering came from a deep-down sickness in my heart. I wondered how it might have been if Naomi and I had married right away instead of running the streets together for eight years first, having our babies without a home to take them to . . .

I thought things would be better when we finally got married, but they weren't. I kept on getting into trouble, more than ever, and spent more time *in* jail than out of it. Naomi was left by herself to do the best she could for the children.

Our "home" was a tiny bedroom at her mother's apartment, more like a closet really, with one window, stuff piled to the ceiling in every corner, and nothing but a dusty old drape for a door. The only light came from a naked bulb dangling from the flaking plaster ceiling. There was a flyspecked cord to pull it off and on. We could hardly move around in there for junk toppling down on us, trash that nobody wanted. Breathing wasn't easy either, with the ugly stained mattress and the worn bedclothes holding the stink of everything that had ever happened there. And we never dared to leave the baby, because of the rats— *What would it have been like if we'd had our own place, some place we really belonged, if—*

But it was too late to think about that now.

"Say, what day is it?" I called to Charlie, the con next to me. I could hardly recognize my own voice, my throat was so filled up with sadness. I knew suddenly that I had to see Nay one more time, even if she *was* dead.

"Dunno," he answered. "Monday mebbe? Visitin' day yestiddy?"

I counted on my fingers. It wasn't easy to keep the

days apart. The sameness made them all kind of run together, like rain in puddles when the storm sewers got clogged up with trash.

Besides, I didn't like to think about the time when I was in jail. If I didn't keep track too close, sometimes I'd lose a day and be that much closer to the time when I'd be out. I didn't want to look at the clock, not even at the top line of a newspaper. TV was better—it didn't name the date all the time. I didn't want to rush away the time, like six months of my life. I didn't want it all gone, but I did always look forward to the day I'd be out, especially when my time was getting short.

"Ain't it Monday?" My man's question brought me back.

"Yeah," I nodded, figuring he was probably right about it. "Hey, I need to make some 'rangements right away!" I broke out of line to approach the hack. His hand flew to the blackjack on his hip, his face never changing.

"Naw, don't get worried," I explained. "I'm not tryin' to start nuthin'—but I gotta see the warden right away. My wife's gonna be buried. Hafta git out and go to her funeral!"

I could tell the hack was listening, and he seemed to be on my side, like he wanted me to go. He let me see the warden as soon as another roller came to relieve him.

"It's okay with us, Miles," the warden said, sitting in his prison office behind the big desk with its orderly piles of official-looking papers. "But I'll have to call her family to make sure it's all right with them. That's one of our rules, you understand."

I couldn't see why it had to be. After all, Nay was my wife.

Waiting for the warden to have his secretary dial the number, I kept telling myself that I had left Nay because I loved her, so that she and the kids could have a better chance, a better hold on life. It wasn't good for them to have me, a drug addict of a husband and a father, dragging them down all the time, beating on them, knocking them around for this and that, and stealing from them every chance I got. It just wasn't good for us to be together. So I had the decency to leave her. After all, I didn't love her to beat on her.

When she asked me for a divorce and I said yes, she broke down and cried.

"Whatcha doin' that for?" I asked her. "I'm just agreein' to what you say you want."

"Yeah, I know it," she said. "And the guy I'm gonna marry is gonna pay for the divorce. So what *am* I cryin' about?"

We both laughed then, on the outside, and went into a bar to have a drink to celebrate. But Naomi never did let the divorce go all the way through.

I wondered if the warden could understand all that. *She was always awful good to me,* I wanted to tell him. *Never troubled me for support of the kids, never called the law no matter what I did—even when I beat her half to death—wouldn't let none of her folks put me away neither—*

For a minute I was brimful of love for the whole world, and then I heard the warden say, "Sorry, Floyd," as he hung up the telephone and shoved it away from him.

"Sorry? Whatcha mean, sorry?" I asked. "Ya mean I can't go?"

He nodded. I was more surprised than mad at first.

"Ya sure?" I asked.

"Yep," he explained, standing up to let me know there wasn't any need to try to talk him into forgetting the rules. "Your mother-in-law doesn't want her grandchildren to see their daddy in handcuffs, she says."

Not want her grandchildren to see me in handcuffs! Hell! I could see through that. It wasn't the children she was concerned about. It was her friends and neighbors. She didn't want *them* to know. She was thinking I wasn't a good-enough husband for her daughter, she—

Man, how could she! Hot blood rushed to my head, and suddenly all the pent-up grief and love and loneliness inside me hardened into mad-dog fury. If I could have gotten my hands on my mother-in-law, I'd have choked her to death.

I wanted to lunge at the desk, to take my hate out on the telephone, to strangle every voice that had ever told me no. If I'd thought I could get by with it, I'd have grabbed the phone and hurled it at the wall.

The hack, who was watching me the whole time, sensed what was happening inside me.

"Cool it, Floyd, cool it," he ordered. But I couldn't cool it. I was mad as hell, so mad I could feel the blood pounding in my head, and I saw whirling stars spinning like crazy before my eyes.

I'd seen stars like that once before . . .

Chapter II

It was two days before Christmas. All Harlem had come alive with the season. Records blared "Jingle Bells" from the corner drugstore. Old ladies dragged loaded shopping bags down the crowded sidewalks; red and green gift-wrapped bargains decorated every barred storefront window; and tired shouts of "Merry Christmas! Ho! Ho! Ho!" came from the lean bellies of scraggly-bearded, toothless, Salvation Army Santa Clauses.

The air was full of good smells—from big piles of shiny red apples, towers of golden oranges, and rows of green-needled Christmas trees lying in the streets, waiting to be sold.

Overhead on 125th Street, in the main shopping

area that we called the capital city of Harlem, there were long strings of beautiful colored lights. They made it look like it was the capital of the whole world.

I was enjoying the great celebration, sitting on the crumbling steps in front of a brownstone apartment. The windows were boarded up, the garbage cans gone from their place in front of the house, and the soot lay heavy on the front stoop. The house was deserted and lonely looking. But I wasn't lonely. The whiskey inside me kept me company, warming and friendly.

On the sidewalk halfway down the block two mangy spotted dogs were growling and scrapping over a bone from the garbage scattered there. I watched them for a little, then whistled, and one jumped away looking hurt, like I had hit him with a slingshot. He tucked his tail between his legs, and went back to sniffing and pawing through the trash for some other tidbit. He seemed so pitiful, so uncomfortable with his head cocked at an awkward angle so he could keep an eye on me, that I had to laugh out loud.

"I ain't gonna hurt you none, dog," I said. "Matter of fact, I might getcha a bone—"

I set my almost empty whiskey bottle on the steps beside me and stood up to turn my pockets inside out to see if I had any money, any pennies even, that I might have overlooked.

Nothing. Coat pockets had a few crumbs of tobacco, some worthless scraps of paper, a couple of rubber bands, and a beer-can opener. Pants' pockets had a key to my mother's apartment, a hair comb, a pocket knife, my empty billfold, and a screwdriver I had copped from a five-and-ten-cent store, slipping it up the sleeve of my coat when nobody was looking. I could feel my mouth turn down in disappointment, being sorry I didn't have anything for the mutt. Then I remembered something.

"Don'tcha worry none, dog," I said, staggering over to him and patting him on the head. "My boss, Mr. Bethel, he owes me a little scratch, and I'm aimin' to go git it—right now. Then me and you can have us a party!"

I'd asked my boss at Parkview Cleaners on St. Nicholas Avenue to save some of my wages back for me from my job as a presser in his tailoring shop, so I'd be sure to have some spending money for Christmas. I could collect the money whenever I wanted it. I wanted it now, and it was just sitting there, waiting for me.

"Don't run off—'cause I'll be right back," I said, whistling at the dog again and laughing when he perked up his stubby ears. I took a last long swig from my bottle and sent it crashing into the gutter. Swiping the back of my hand across my lips, I started down the sidewalk, a little unsteady, kicking up a clatter of beer cans as I went.

It had turned cold enough that people were thinning out in the neighborhood, getting inside where it was warm and they could be out of the wind. But I was so happy I must have thought it was summertime. I side-stepped the trash-littered piles of dirty gray snow, shoved at garbage cans lined up against the ghetto apartments, and stopped to read every word of the sexy posters plastered against the girlie-show theaters along the way.

I hadn't gone more than three blocks when a wind as cold as hate picked up a carload of gritty dirt and dumped it in my eyes with a fierce stinging vengeance. *Man, how it hurt!*

I backed against the side of a fence and stopped to let my eyes water themselves clean. The pain was so bad I wanted to quit walking, to get inside somewhere myself. Only I wanted some scratch first.

Hey! No need for me to go all that way to get a little bread, nohow, I realized suddenly. *No sense to that at all. Why, there's bound to be somethin' closer at hand, somethin' I can get without so much trouble.*

But the cars parked along the edge of the street were empty. There were no overcoats or other stuff left lying in the seats as far as I could see. I didn't want to take off a tire to sell, or strip chrome, or anything like that, because I was sharp—all dressed up in a new coat. I didn't want to get it messed up. I stroked my lapels as I walked on, enjoying the feel of them as I looked around for a chance to make a quick sting.

And then I saw it—a dark little corner grocery store across the street, a store with heavy steel grids on the windows but just a pane of glass in the door—no wires, no nothing. There was no sign of a burglar alarm. I could bust in so easy. How stupid could they get? It was like a big welcome mat, a "help yourself" sign. Actually, I was so juiced up with whiskey I didn't care anyway. I'd probably have tried to break into Fort Knox if it'd been handy.

I darted across the street, detouring around a green car left in the middle of the intersection with a flat tire and leaping over the ugly dirty snow in the gutters. Taking a carelessly quick look up and down the street and deciding that no one was paying any attention to me, I was ready to go.

It didn't take half a second for me to lift the battered lid from an overflowing garbage can and hurl it at the glass in the door with all my strength behind it. Slivers of glass flew like sparks in a welding shop, and bigger chunks of glass crashed to the floor inside. The racket pushed my head down inside the collar of my new camel's-hair coat, and I scrunched my shoulders up to protect my ears from the sound, almost as if I thought that would keep anyone else from hearing it.

When everything was quiet, I glanced up and down the street and saw that it was clear; no one was in sight. It looked like I was home free. I danced over the bottom of the doorframe and was safely inside the store.

It was gloomy in there, what with the gray day outdoors and the bars shading the windows. I had to strain my eyes to make out anything in the dark.

There oughtta be a cash register somewhere, I thought, spotting it immediately, over on the lefthand counter, just past a squared-off pile of loaves of bread. I tiptoed over and was reaching my hand into the drawer when I heard a long shrill whistle and running feet.

The man! I whirled and grabbed the handle of a big walk-in icebox and slid inside, pulling the door shut behind me. I crouched there shivering in the cold lonesome darkness, hardly daring to breathe. I couldn't hear a thing from the outside, because the thudding of my heart was booming as loud as twin locomotives getting up steam for a race. That had happened to me more than many times. I waited for the cops to leave, holding my teeth tightly clenched to keep them from chattering like castanets. It seemed like I waited forever.

Suddenly a blinding shaft of light hit me full in the face when the big door swung open and three cops confronted me, two white and one black.

"All right, you," the big one holding the spotlight growled. "Out! Out!"

I knew they had me. There was no use protesting, no point in going into my "I'm innocent" act, so I was ready to look sad, pitiful like a wet puppy, and throw myself on their mercy.

Raising my hands high above my head, I started toward them, ducking the waxy red sides of beef and the looping strings of speckled sausages hanging in the refrigerator. My ducking must have looked suspicious, like I was trying to resist arrest, because the next thing I knew, the big cop had grabbed the back of my coat and was dragging me fast across the dark oiled wooden floor and out onto the broken sidewalk. Then he jerked me upright, and I saw the jack in his hand. His arm went up and down again and again as I felt my knees folding, and I sank into a heap, like a slapstick comic in a slow-motion moving picture.

I was so drunk I didn't feel a thing, not even when my eyes saw stars whirling crazily before them. I didn't realize I'd been hit until I saw a dark spreading stain on the lapels of my beautiful new coat. Where was it coming from?

Puzzled, I put my hand to my head and felt the warm sticky blood spurting out from the side of it. I still didn't feel any physical hurt—but mentally, it was torture. *My coat! My beautiful new coat!* I'd always loved nice clothes, and it made me mad as hell that the crummy cop had spoiled my coat.

"You stinkin' S.O.B.'s!" I cussed them. "You no good dirty slobs!" I stared at the blood on my hand, and then I began to cry, great heaving sobs. By that time a crowd had gathered. They were deathly still as they looked from me to the bulls and back again.

I couldn't stand the quiet, so I screamed, waving my bloody hand at the onlookers. And then I called the cops every vile, filthy name I could think of. But no one joined me. I was hoping somebody would pity me, sympathize, and at least say, "I'm sorry," but nobody seemed to care.

The big cop lifted me to my feet—feet that didn't want to stay under me—and somebody in the crowd snickered as he shoved my powerless body into the wagon, jammed my wobbly legs in after me, slammed the door, and took off for the precinct. I felt funny, riding in the police car; I knew I didn't belong there.

I was seventeen. I had never been arrested for anything before in my life.

Chapter III

"What's the charge?" the grizzled desk sergeant wanted to know, sounding as tired and looking as worn out as a split-open inner tube.

"Breaking and entering. Attempted burglary. Resisting arrest," the big officer barked at him, sending a disgusted look in my direction.

Resisting arrest? My mind fumbled around the word, trying to protest, but my mouth refused to open.

The sergeant asked more questions as he filled in the blanks of the important-looking papers in front of him, but I didn't hear them all. It took every bit of brain I had to keep me on my feet. My knees wanted to bend the wrong way, and the floor wouldn't hold still. My head was beginning to beat painfully, in time to some weird calypso music inside itself. I just wanted to curl up somewhere and die. But every time I shut my eyes, a blazing ball of fire shot daggers of searing torture into my head. I couldn't stand it.

"Anybody you want to call?" The question blurred through the fog in my mind. "ANYBODY YOU WANT TO CALL?" The desk sergeant had to shout at me twice before I realized he was expecting me to answer.

I heard myself mumble my sister Mary's telephone number, and then the big officer half dragged me, half shoved me along outside into the wagon for a fast ride to the hospital. He jerked me out of the car, pushed me down a long corridor reeking of antiseptic, kicked open a door labeled "Emergency Only," and dropped me into a chair beside a white-papered table. He backed against the opposite wall and stayed there, his legs spread-eagled, his eyes never leaving me. A crisply starched nurse nudged me onto the table, sprayed a local anesthetic onto my still dripping head, and shaved it so a rumpled young intern could stitch me up. He didn't say a word during the whole operation. Except for muffled sounds that filtered through the walls—once I thought I heard a dog yipping like he was in pain—the room was silent the whole time with only the heavy sound of my breathing and the whispered scratching of the nurse's razor.

When the intern had finished, he spoke a curt,

"Okay, he's all yours," to the police who drove me back to the precinct, prodded me back into the building and down a short passageway to a cell, clanging the door shut behind me.

I collapsed on the spot and didn't remember anything until a few hours later when a wary guard, smaller than I was, kicked me in the side.

"Get on up there!" he muttered in a deep-throated voice when I blinked up at him, trying to make out where I was. It looked like jail, but I knew I didn't belong in jail—

He jerked his head down the hallway to the left.

"Time to go home," he said. "Yer sister paid fer ya." He spat the words out, making it sound like she had committed a capital offense.

I picked myself up, lurched against the cold steel of the bars of the cell, steadied myself, and shuffled out in the direction he indicated. He followed at a safe distance and told me where to turn.

"Bunky, whatsa matter, whatsa matter?" My sister shook her head and wrung her hands when I walked into the cold, ugly waiting room of the precinct. I thought she was going to pass out when she saw the blood on my head and clothes. "What hit ya?" she cried as she weaved across the room to touch my arm. I felt her sorrow, her embarrassment and shame settling down like a soft pillow, smothering me. Unable to make myself face the hurt in her eyes, I counted the cracks between the boards on the floor.

"What hit ya?" she asked again.

"A dude bust me in the head," I mumbled to her, finally, and we started out the door together.

"Don'tcha look for him back," she called over her well-rounded shoulder as we headed out to the sidewalk, her hand steadying my still unreliable steps. "Floyd ain't never been in no trouble before—he ain't that kind of a boy. Ya can look at yore record—ain't none of his brothers and sisters never been mixed up with the law neither."

My head was sober enough by that time to realize that she was really telling *me* instead of the other people in the station. The truth sinking in made my head hang still lower, the disgrace putting more weight onto the pain already in it.

Mary took me home with her, warning me about what my stepfather might do when he found out I'd been in trouble.

"Bunky, ya don't hafta take no lip offa him," she said, as she gently washed off the dried blood staining my neck and shoulders and brought me a clean shirt. "Don't worry about it. An' don't let him hit ya neither. Remember—he ain't yore *real* daddy."

I had heard it all before—a million times while I was growing up. I'd never seen my real father, not to know who I was looking at. He and my mother just couldn't make it together somehow, and I lived mostly with my grandmother and my great-grandmother until I was old enough to go to school. Then I had to get used to my mother on a day-to-day basis and try to fit into her new family with my three half-sisters and a half-brother.

"What shall I call him, Mama," I asked, the first day when my stepfather left to go to work.

"Why, call him Dad, Bunky, like the other children do," she said, kind of hugging me to her as she gave me my sweater and a nickel for some candy.

My grandmother, who was standing in the kitchen washing dishes, overheard us and poked her head into the hallway, sudsy water dripping from her elbows.

"Naw, Bunky," she rasped, her voice hoarse with a cold. "He ain't yore daddy. Don'tcha call him nuthin'!" It made me sad to hear her say that. Because if he wasn't my daddy, then I didn't belong to him. And she never let me forget it.

Whenever I did something wrong and my stepfather raised the devil with me, my grandmother got upset about it.

"He got no right to hit you, Bunky," she reminded me time after time. "I bet he don't hit them other young 'uns that he's got. Remember—don't never fergit it—he ain't yore real daddy."

She shook her head as she sided with me, no matter how wrong I was, and I felt a big lump of resentment swelling up inside my chest, hurting like a chunk of meat I hadn't chewed long enough before I swallowed it. The resentment kept me feeling separated from the rest of my family, like I didn't belong with any of them. My brothers and sisters and I weren't as close to one another as we should have been.

But sometimes I knew better, like the day I carried my stepfather's lunch to him where he worked as a racker in a pool hall. He kind of patted me on the head when I handed him the brown bag with the plate of fried chicken, potatoes, and biscuits still warm from the oven.

"Thank you, son," he said, and then he hollered out for everyone around the green felt table to hear:

"Hey, you guys! This here's my boy—my Floyd!" They unbent from their cues and smiled at me, making me feel warm inside, like I'd just had a big mug of hot cocoa. And all the way home I kept telling myself, "He didn't say, 'This here's my *wife's* boy'; he said 'This here's *my* boy!' and he acted happy about it, like he felt it too, the good feeling, the belonging to each other."

Sometimes I wished my grandmother would quit reminding me that he wasn't my real daddy. Then I could forget it, and just sink in and belong to the love in our house—all the time. But she didn't quit. Not ever.

When I was little we lived in a five-room apartment in Harlem, and there was a lot of happiness there. Families were close to one another, visiting a lot. There was a little game we kids played. I'd tag a friend on the shoulder and holler, "Partners," and then I got to go home with him and eat and sleep at his house.

The next day he might get slick and beat me to the tap so he could come home and eat with me.

I used to like to play partners with a boy named Merlin Minor. His mother was from down south, and she was always cooking something good—southern fried chicken, country ham, and soft biscuits to sop in the gravy. There was lots of sticky sweet molasses to eat with biscuits, too. I had to be careful not to wear out my welcome at Merlin's house. I knew it wouldn't be right for me to go every day. I held myself back, so his mama wouldn't get tired of me and make me stop going altogether.

Food was one of the important things in life, and we were always looking for something good to eat. If we saw a friend coming out of his place with a piece of cake or slab of apple pie, we'd call out "haggies" and he'd have to divide it with us.

There was always enough to eat, even when things were pretty tight and the icebox was empty. Soul food—fried potatoes, fatback, blackeyed peas, syrup, cabbage, potatoes, and cornbread—kept us fat as butterballs.

And everybody in Harlem was always expecting to strike it rich—get a new pair of shoes, a big pot of money, a fur coat, or a Cadillac—from the favorite form of gambling, playing the numbers. The dream of hittin' that number was a little hope to brighten up our days. We saved a quarter out of every dollar, sometimes as much as seventy-five cents—even when we were on welfare—to give to our number man at the candy store. Some families would save a quarter to eat with and spend all the rest with the number man.

One morning when my Aunt Betty was staying with us, she woke up all excited and got dressed before breakfast to go to the candy store to see the number man. She was so happy that I tagged along just to see what she was up to.

It was so early she had to pound on the door to get Joe to open up for her.

"Kinda early, ain'tcha?" he asked, rubbing his eyes when he let her in. I'd never seen him before without his false teeth. His bristly turned-up chin almost hit his nose when he talked. I watched him, fascinated.

"I'm too excited to wait, Joe," my aunt told him. "Had me a dream las' night, that I was gonna move to a house number 763. I just know that's gonna be my lucky number this week."

She fished in her bosom, drew out a knotted handkerchief, and counted out six limp dollar bills and handed them to him.

"Play 763 for me for sixty cents combination and forty cents straight for a week," she said, like she knew what she was doing.

Joe twitched his nose around and raised his eyebrows a little.

"Ya sure ya don't wanna split it up and keep somethin' on yore reg'lar lucky number?" he asked. His nose and chin almost *banged* together that time.

"Naw," she said. "This here's right. I just *know* it is."

Joe shook his head at her as if he didn't think women had much sense. He glared at me for staring at him, fished his false teeth from his hip pocket and clacked them into place. Then he wrote her new number in the little black number pad he always carried in his hand so he could get rid of it in a hurry if the man came down on him.

People usually learned the winning number from listening to the radio; they didn't have to wait for the afternoon paper to hit the streets. But our radio was broken, and so every afternoon that week, my aunt threw up the window of our third floor apartment and hollered down to the folks on the sidewalk:

"What is it? Have you heard? What'd they do? What's the last one? What's the second one? What's the first one?"

And when someone hollered back to her 369 or 264 or 798 she just saw, "Aww! Well, tomorra will be the day—" And she acted like she believed it.

She kept on believing it until Saturday when the winning number was the one she *usually* played, 242, her *old* house number. A dream had cost her six dollars plus the six hundred she might have won. Aunt Betty never played anything *but* her old house number after that, but it was never a winner again.

We all needed something like the numbers to keep our minds off the dirt and filth, the wretchedness around us. Our physical surroundings were too awful to think about.

Big brown roaches scurried for a dark corner

whenever we moved a piece of furniture or turned on a light in a room at night. And there were water rats as big as cats nesting all around us. Often we heard of families where the babies were deathly sick from rat bites. One morning when a woman in our block went to look at her baby girl sleeping in a carriage, she found bloody blankets and a baby that wouldn't breathe again. Rats were always hungry, and they were everywhere.

When I was a little boy still living with my grandmother, I was in the kitchen one morning watching her fry some potatoes in hot grease. A sudden gust of wind blew the window curtains toward the stove, knocking a salt box into the skillet of bubbling fat. It splattered all over the place. I hollered at the top of my lungs, blistered in half-a-dozen tiny spots where the flying grease had hit my face and arms. In two seconds the stove was blazing.

"Lord! Fire! Fire!" my grandmother screamed, grabbing my hand and racing down the hallway to the living room where the window opened above the busy street three stories below. She leaned halfway out, with me clinging to her hand for dear life, and yelled, "Fire! Fire! Fire!" at a bunch of neighborhood kids playing in the spray of a fire hydrant. They heard her and took off at a fast gallop toward the fire station in the next block. Then, with me still clutching her hand, she yelled, "Come on, Bunky," and flew with me into the front bedroom. I didn't think there was anything in there worth saving, but she snatched open the closet door and grabbed one of her white dresses off a hanger, jamming it into a shopping bag with her white straw hat and the white shoes and stockings she always wore to church. My grandmother wouldn't have known how to live without her white Sunday clothes.

Black smoke choked the narrow hallway as we tumbled down the stairs, getting out as fast as we could. The stairwell was a dark raceway of people scrambling over each other, hurrying to safety with whatever they had grabbed up—a lamp, an iron, a blanket, a Bible, a picture of a boy in uniform—when they heard the dreaded cry through their open windows.

The fire truck arrived almost as soon as we reached the street, its shrieking siren splitting our ears. Red-coated firemen swarmed like ants, getting a ladder against the building, turning off the hydrant so they could attach their hoses onto it, and carrying hoses and fire extinguishers up the wobbling ladder to our front window where smoke was billowing out. A gang of noisy neighbors jammed the sidewalks, offering advice and getting in the way. While the firemen were working, a steady stream of rats poured from the building, seeking safety in adjoining apartments or disappearing down the sewer openings along the street.

When the fire was out and we went back into the smoke-blackened kitchen, we were surprised that it wasn't all burned up. The stove was ruined, but the shelves above it were still usable; the icebox was black, but the door would open and shut. I couldn't make out the pictures on the tin cans of food on the counter, but none of the cans had burst.

My aunt Mary, whose sense of humor helped to keep life worth living even when times were bad, said she knew why the damage was not worse.

"I'll tell you why the fire got put out so fast," she said. "You heard that army of rats squeaking when they came scattering out of the house when the firemen were getting the hose ready?" We nodded, wondering what was coming next. "Well," she explained, "they were saying, 'Hurry up! Get this fire out so we can get back in our house!' And the rats were so big the firemen *had* to hurry. They were scared to death." She doubled over in a loud guffaw, slapping her ample thighs.

I looked at her with my mouth hanging wide open, my eyes popping at the wonder of it. It really *was* like the house belonged to the rats instead of the people. Many times I'd be taking a nap on a bed or couch in the daytime and hear a scratching noise and open my eyes to see a huge gray-brown rat or two, big as squirrels, nibbling at crumbs or papers within an arm's reach of me.

"Get outta here!" I'd yell, and maybe throw a shoe at them. Sometimes, if I had a slingshot in my pocket, I'd shoot at them with wads of paper.

It wasn't just the rats and roaches that made a Harlem apartment bad to live in. There were smells too, smells that never quit. The dirty hallways, with broken bottles, discarded boxes, and other kinds of trash crowded into every corner, stank of garbage, urine, and stale cigarettes, of burned beans, of garlic, vomit, and baby diapers. We kids made a game of it sometimes, taking a deep breath before we went into our building to see if we could keep from breathing in again until we were inside our own apartment. There was no such thing as fresh air even there, but sometimes a good smell, like barbecued spareribs, or boiled chitlins, or pickled pigs' feet, was strong enough to overpower the bad ones. Even a breeze through the windows was more likely to carry the stench of rotting garbage, human waste, or a dead cat than a good smell like spring rain.

Our apartments were never comfortable. In winter we'd huddle for warmth around the heating stove or a clanking radiator. For fuel we used whatever we could scrounge off the streets or pry from boarded-up windows along dark alleys. In the summer, we suffocated. Open windows brought in more heat from the steaming streets and rooftops as well as all the loud arguments of people who were as out-of-sorts as the weather. Folks on welfare like we were most of the time couldn't afford an electric fan big enough to do any good. Sometimes we'd crawl out the window and sleep on the fire escape or carry an old mattress or some sofa pillows up to the roof after the sun had been down long enough for the black tar to give up most of its heat.

The roofs and fire escapes were our playgrounds

too, along with the littered backyards, the abandoned cars lining every street, and the condemned broken-windowed apartments where no one was supposed to live.

We had good-natured fights, just throwing garbage can lids at each other, and, although none of us had regular spending money, we had parties all the time. We stole mickeys and potatoes from the neighborhood grocery store and cooked them over bonfires in the backyards. Or we'd break into a candy store to get treats to eat.

Jumping from one rooftop to another was our favorite sport almost all year round. None of us realized the awful danger of it until the summer when I was thirteen.

Half a dozen of us fellows and a tomboy girl were out one night having a daredevil time, playing follow-the-leader on the rooftops in our neighborhood. I never liked jumping roofs. Just leaning over the edge and looking down five stories to the street was enough to make my stomach turn flips. The big space between the buildings, sometimes as much as eight feet wide, scared me till I felt pale inside. But I didn't want to be left out. I had to belong to the gang. I didn't want the other guys to think I was afraid—and I didn't want myself to think so either.

So I got in line, behind some of the others, and I backed way up when it was my turn to jump. I got a good running start and worked up plenty of speed. Still, sometimes I had to cut it off, putting the brakes on hard when I reached the edge of the roof and knew I couldn't make it. My sneakers made a stretched out track in the soft tar of the rooftop when I stopped suddenly. And I had to turn around and try again. It was always worse to do it the second time. My stomach dropped to my toes, and my heart was in my mouth as my feet thudded into the neighboring rooftop. Then I relaxed for a minute waiting for the last jumpers to catch up. I could tell some of the others were scared too. But we tried not to show our scaredness to each other. We all used to lie about it.

"I ain't jumpin' that one," I said, about eleven o'clock one night when the kids were lining up to jump between my apartment building at 352 St. Nicholas and the corner house at 309 on the other street.

"Whatsa matter, Bunky, ya scared?" my friend Roy asked me. He lived at 350, just next door.

"Naw, I ain't scared," I lied. "I just ain't gonna jump no more tonight, that's all." I yawned, pretending to be sleepy, and went downstairs to my apartment after detouring to wake up the pigeons one of the boys was keeping in a cage on the roof.

"Didja hear about Roy?" my friend Snooky asked me next day, looking more serious than I'd ever seen him.

"*Hear* about Roy?" I laughed. "Man, I seen him!" That Roy is undoubtly the loosest jointedest, the wobbliest, the biggest clown of a acrobat I ever saw. Don't guess he's ever been scared of nuthin'," I said.

"He was still jumpin' strong last night when I quit and went home."

Then I noticed Snooky's face. He wasn't laughing with me. He wasn't even smiling.

"Hey, what's wrong?" I wanted to know. "Roy couldn't be hurt—could he?" Snooky's face made me wonder. "He couldn't be hurt—he's a born acrobat," I insisted.

"Yeah," Snooky agreed, his voice rasping as he ground his knuckles into his eyelids, "he sure was."

"Was?" Suddenly I felt all hollow inside.

"Roy tried to jump too far last night—right after you left—" Snooky went on, sort of whispering. "It was awful—he din't make it—fell between the corner house and—" His voice broke and he stopped to clear his throat. "He grabbed holt to that pipe on the way down, the big chimney pipe, tried to hold on—but—"

Snooky stopped again and I waited, holding my breath. In my mind I could see the fat chimney pipe going down the side of the building. And I tried to imagine Roy pressing into it, trying to hang on, spreading his arms wide to reach partway around it, with nothing to grip onto. Maybe he tried to put his legs around too. I felt my muscles straining, figuring how to hang on for him, knowing there'd be no way anyone could do it for long. I shuddered and caught my breath, feeling myself slipping down even as I tried, picturing how awful it must have been for him.

"Couldn't you git to him out a window?" I pleaded,

the tears welling up inside me, my fists clenching together so tight my fingernails bit into the skin.

"No windows on that side," Snooky reminded me in a flat, helpless voice.

For a minute we both stood in hopeless silence, our grief joining together in the middle of it.

"We got to the street just after he hit," Snooky whispered, his eyes widening, the horror growing in him as he relived the scene. "He was sayin', 'Pipe too hot, pipe too hot . . .' You could almost smell how burned he was." Snooky shivered. "There was black streaks of soot down the front of his shirt, and the inside of his arms . . . Somebody ran to git his mama but she din't get there quick enough—"

"From five stories up?" I gulped, counting the windows in my mind. Snooky nodded, his Adam's apple bobbing up and down as he kept trying to swallow.

"Then you mean—he didn't make it at all—he's dead?" My voice trailed off in an adolescent squeak. I knew the answer already, in every inch of my body. But it was like I had to hear the word "dead" out loud to begin to understand that it was true.

"I seen him from the edge of the roof just before he turned loose of the pipe," Snooky whispered hoarsely shaking his head. "His knuckles had turned right white where he was trying to hold on—the pipe was that hot. And just before he let go he screamed, like he knowed he had to hold on—or die—but—"

Snooky stopped and buried his face in his hands. I tried to imagine what it would be like, being so fried I had to let go, falling so far, the hard ground rushing up to break me, to pound a new kind of pain into me. It was too real.

All of a sudden I was cold, stone cold. So cold it didn't seem like the fires of hell itself could ever warm me.

Snooky's shoulders were heaving up and down. He sobbed like he'd never stop.

I never jumped the roofs again after that. Belonging wasn't that important.

Chapter IV

One sweltering August afternoon when I was fourteen I was hanging around a corner candy store with a couple of my friends. Merlin, a boy I'd known all my life, had jackknifed himself—all six feet of him—on the steps where he was thumping a pair of bongo drums in time to the piccolo music blaring from the candy store.

Brother, as plump and high-yellow as Merlin was black and skinny, was dancing a jig in time to the music. His feet flew, the heel and toe plates on his shoes click-clacking in perfect rhythm as his upraised arms made a dance of their own. His rusty white T-shirt and dark green pants fit him as tight as sausage skin, so there was no flopping shirttail or pant legs to spoil the picture. His motions were as smooth and unwrinkled as thick molasses pouring out of a jug.

I sat on the sidewalk hugging my knees, my back pressed hard against the sunbaked side of the steps, the dry heat of the concrete feeling good to my sweaty body. When it was awfully hot, sometimes I'd quit trying to fight the heat and just let myself melt into it. It seemed to help someway.

Across St. Nicholas Avenue some kids were doing their thing for the crowds that swarmed by, going nowhere in particular. My ears were happy soaking up the music, being part of the scene, and I moved my head in time to the beat. Watching Brother, I wished I had some talent for something myself, like I saw in so many other people. Then maybe someday I could have the things I read about in the school books, things like rich folks had . . .

A big double-decker bus full of white sightseers stopped at the corner, and a man with a clipped black poodle in his arms got off. He didn't belong to our neighborhood, that was for sure. He was sharp looking, wearing gray spats and a bright blue derby hat. He hooked a leash to the dog's harness, put him down, and walked over to watch Brother dance. The dog stood still for a minute, then lay down, resting his head on his front paws, looking like he'd be content to stay forever.

After a few minutes, the man dropped the leash to the sidewalk and stuck his hand in the pocket of his bright red vest, taking out a handful of coins and holding them out toward Brother. He wound up his dance with a staccato flourish and took the coins, dividing them with Merlin who unfolded his lanky form to stand up and put his share in his pants' pocket. I watched a dime roll and fall through a sidewalk grating.

"Wonder why that dog was restin' so easy, not tryin' to git away, when the man didn't have a hold on him," Merlin said, as the dog and the man disappeared around the corner. "Looks to me like he missed a good chance to be free—" Merlin was chomping at the bit, impatient for freedom when it looked to me like he already had all the freedom there was. He'd been on his own for a couple of years already.

"Dogs just plain don't have no sense, no sense a-tall," Brother puffed, leaning against the building to catch up on his breathing.

"Man, that ain't it," I said. "Can'tcha see? I was watchin' him the whole time. Man, that dog, he's already free. That leash ain't holdin' him nowhere. He's right where he wants to be—with the one he belongs to, the one who takes care of him and feeds him and looks out for him so bigger dogs won't eat him up or cars run over him—" The more I thought about it, the more I knew that dog really had it made. Wanting to belong to someone was something I thought about a lot, because I never exactly felt like I did. Freedom? Well, I probably already had all the freedom I could handle, more than was good for me.

Like I had decided not to go back to school when it opened in two weeks. Years when I had lots of bronchitis and pneumonia had put me so far behind in school that I had failed my grade a couple of times. My younger brothers and sisters had got ahead of me, and since I was so much bigger, it made me look like a dummy. I had skipped school more times than not the year before, and I'd have to stay in the sixth grade again if I went back. I couldn't see doing that, staying with the babies and me already fifteen and crowding six feet tall. I didn't belong there.

Sitting there thinking, wondering where I did belong, I fished in my shirt pocket for a collapsed pack of cigarettes. I took out the last one, crumpled the package, and tossed it into the gutter where it floated on top of the scummy water left standing after the morning thunderstorm, the water dammed up by the sodden trash in the street. The day felt like it was shaping up for another storm if it didn't cool off pretty soon. The air was as heavy as a mattress left out in the rain.

"Got another cigarette I can have?" I asked Brother when mine was too short to keep smoking. I knew Merlin didn't smoke.

"Naw," he said, "my old lady found my hidin' place and got rid of all my smokes yesterday. I din't have no scratch to git me some more."

I wasn't supposed to be smoking either, and I didn't mean to get caught at it. My mother had gone to work—she usually worked on Tuesdays, ironing for some white lady with half-a-dozen kids. And my stepfather had a job too, for a change, WPA road work. I wasn't looking for him to be in the neighborhood till late suppertime, and it was still early enough that I could reach to the end of my shadow without hardly trying.

I pushed myself up to a standing position so I could check my pockets to make sure I hadn't overlooked a cigarette somehow.

"Well, whadaya know?" I exclaimed, discovering a half-smoked roach in my pocket. "I still got somethin' to puff after all." I lit it and stood there smoking the piece of cigarette, inhaling to get all the good out of it.

All of a sudden, without any warning, my stepfather strode around the corner, a newspaper tucked under his arm. It was folded to the want ads, like maybe he'd lost his job again and been out looking for a new one.

"Bunk!"

BOP!

I felt him hit me almost before I saw him, he was that fast. He slapped me hard, bashed me right in the mouth, roasting his hand on the lit cigarette, nearly making me swallow the butt.

"Wait a sec—" I cried out, ducking his fist when it shot out again. "That wasn't no reef—just a plain ole cigarette." I knew he thought I was smoking marijuana. But the longer I explained, the madder he got, and he busted me on the side of the head again.

Later, when he had calmed down and he and my mother had talked about it, he was sorry he'd been so rough.

"If yer gonna smoke, Bunky," he said, "ya might

just as well do it out in the open. No need to sneak off and hide somewheres, or to wait till I'm outta sight. I won't never hit ya fer it again." And he never did. Maybe, if he'd been my real daddy, he'd have helped me straighten up and made me stay in school. But he didn't—I guess he knew I didn't belong to him.

My life started crashing downhill from that day on, like a gigantic landslide I didn't have the power to stop. If I could get permission to smoke by being caught smoking, I figured that I could do anything else I wanted to do too. And it seemed like I just had to be bad. There was nobody to make me be good.

I didn't go back to school; I started drinking and being mixed up with women. I left home to live with a woman old enough to be my mother. And I ran the streets hog wild. I was my own man.

It was then that I began getting drawn into street riots where you had to belong to a gang in order to survive. There were gangs everywhere, east, west, north, and south. Spanish gangs, Italian gangs, black gangs. The Bachelors, the Normans, the Socialists, the Midtowns—too many to name them all. The gangs lived to fight one another. I joined a gang called the Royal Crowns. We fought the Spanish guys, and the Italian guys, and sometimes the Jewish fellows up on the hill, and the blacks fought the blacks. We fought with homemade guns, pistols, knives, pipe, pliers, lye—anything—fighting over the least little bit of an argument, a girl—any kind of foolishness.

One morning we had kind of an appointment to

fight the Terrace gang up on the hill. I went along to keep from being called yellow, but the other gang never showed up. We learned later that they had been delayed by a knock-down, drag-out fist fight among themselves in Central Park.

The gang fight was set again for the following night after dark. Everybody was supposed to be there.

"Man, this is gonna be a good one," a tall black boy with two newspaper-wrapped lengths of galvanized pipe under his arm said to me as we waited for our enemies to show up. "I been readyin' up fer a good fight fer a week now, ever since them no-good s.o.b.'s from the Bronx had it with my woman."

"Yeah, man," I lied. "Me too. An' I'm gonna help ya do 'em in!" My only weapon was a baseball bat I had "borrowed" from my brother. I was hoping I wouldn't have to use it.

We heard them coming up the hill a few minutes later, rattling chains and garbage-can lids, banging them together loud enough to turn your ears inside out. About thirty of us stood up screaming, "Come 'n' git it, ya lousy s.o.b.'s! Come 'n' git what's comin' to ya!" I blew myself up, yelling louder than anybody else, but instead of charging forward with the rest, I fell back and stayed in the rear.

I kept on yelling—to sound tough—and nobody wanted to take me on. I planned it that way, not wanting to bust anybody in the head and not wanting to get hit myself. Then all at once a boy from the enemy gang broke through our ranks and headed straight for me. He was a little guy, fast, but so small I could have squashed him with my big toe. He was howling like an Indian, twirling a murderously heavy chain around his head, just high enough to break my neck if it hit me. I held up my baseball bat to defend myself, to stop the whirling iron links, and suddenly I recognized him.

"Spider!" I yelled. It took him off guard, and the chain stopped its threatening circles and flopped down meekly beside him.

"Aw, man, it's me—Bunky," I said. "We growed up together—don't ya 'member me? I don't wanna hurt ya—"

He'd been hurt already, I could see. His shirt was torn almost to shreds, and there was an ugly knot right in the middle of his forehead.

He looked at me for a second as I moved closer into the golden circle of light from the street lamp. He didn't say a word, but I could see something bright turning on behind the hate in his eyes. Then he wheeled around, started whooping again and twirling his chain as he took off, back toward the thick of the fighting.

I saw one of our guys come up behind him then, a long pipe raised high over his head. I yelled, "Look out!" but he never heard me. The crunch was sickening as his whooping gurgled to a stop in his throat and he smashed to the ground, his face splatting into a puddle of muddy water in the gutter. He just lay there, not moving, and I knew it was too late for me or anyone else to help him.

Everything in my stomach boiled up and poured out onto the ground. After I was completely empty, the dry heaves began, trying to throw my very insides out of me. It was like I didn't even want to belong to the human race anymore.

From then on I tried to look for older guys to hang out with. I had to belong somewhere. The older guys were generally a little milder, a little less likely to be rumbling all the time. They made a groove I could fit into better.

It was in me to want to be good, to find some purpose for living, but I kept on with the bad just the same. There was nothing, no one, to set me straight. My life was rotten with the garbage of it, the drinking, sex, gambling, stealing— Sin in life became the point of life for me.

All through the years it seemed like something was trying to get through to me, something was trying to teach me better. One day, long before I started smoking, I wandered into a drugstore to buy some chewing gum with money I had earned delivering packages for a crippled woman in our building. I wasn't planning to steal anything, but a big pile of cigarette cartons was on the counter right under my nose. Nobody was at the counter, and when I looked around I saw that the clerks were too busy helping other people to be paying any attention to me. I couldn't resist sticking one of the cartons inside the front of my windbreaker.

That night I nearly wore a hole in my cot, tossing and turning, trying to go to sleep. I kept thinking about the cigarettes hidden behind some boxes under my bed; about Dr. Blue, the storeowner who'd always been so friendly to me, giving me candy and gum, balloons and things like that. I'd known Dr. Blue all my life. Every time I shut my eyes, I saw his face smiling at me, his piercing brown eyes looking right through me over the top of his horn-rimmed glasses.

Morning finally came, and as soon as the stores were open I put the carton of cigarettes in a brown paper bag and carried it back to the store. I waited my chance, and when there were no other customers around, I walked up to Dr. Blue and handed the bag to him. It was hard to know what to say—

"Dr. Blue, sir—" I began, and had to stop to clear my throat. He looked in the bag, waiting for me to go on. When his eyes met mine, there was a question in them.

"Yesterday, I—" I said, "well, nobody was looking and I—I wanted to bring them back," I finished lamely, not really explaining what had happened.

"Thanks, son," he said, trying to make it easy for me. "Ya wanna put 'em back where they belong now?" I had the funny feeling that it was harder for him to know than for me to admit that I'd done something wrong. He didn't even bawl me out, and he went out of his way to trust me from then on, being careful *not* to watch me when I was in the store, sending me on errands, and letting me make deliveries for him.

But my conscience got quieter and quieter in the next few years, and then it seemed to fade away altogether. Or maybe I just grew so deaf from doing bad things all the time that I couldn't hear it.

Getting off easy with a suspended sentence after my first arrest didn't teach me to mend my ways either. I kept on stealing like other gang members did, for spending money, partly, but mostly just for the fun of it. There was always someone willing to buy my stolen merchandise, and there were pawnshops wherever I looked, pawnshops that never asked any embarrassing questions.

Less than a month after my first arrest, on a beautiful crisp afternoon when the air was so clear I could actually see blue in the sky, I picked up a smooth rock from a big pile of rubbish alongside a building that was being demolished. I strolled down the sidewalk, smoothing the rock over and over in my hands, thinking it might come in handy for something.

Farther down the street I came to a drugstore that looked closed for the day. There were some winos sprawled on the stoop a few houses away, but they weren't in any condition to interfere with my business. Seemed like they were just trying to sleep it off, like a pack of dogs with full stomachs basking in the sun. The only person with his eyes open was leaning against a mailbox, almost swallowed up in a khaki-colored moth-eaten army greatcoat that flopped around his ankles.

In the next block I could see public school # 157 with a high fence around the deserted playground. Across from that were the midmorning whores parading up and down the sidewalk waiting to catch a trick. I could tell that one of them was Teresa, a girl I knew, in her plaid wool slacks with the tail ends of the long green scarf wound around her neck standing out in the breeze. But she wouldn't rat on me, even if she noticed what I was up to.

I tossed the rock up and down in my hand a few times, getting the heft of it, then chunked it at the drugstore window, but not hard enough. It bounced right off, sounding like a shot but making a hole no bigger than a BB. I picked it back up, wondering why I was trying to break into the store. I couldn't see anything in the window that appealed to me, and I had a week's wages in my pocket. But I didn't have anything else to do, and there was no reason *not* to break in, so —I drew my arm back to throw the rock again, harder this time, and I heard a siren screaming up and saw a big cop bouncing out of the police car right toward me.

I leaned against the side of the building, stuck my hands in my pockets, and started to whistle, trying to pretend that I was completely innocent of any wrongdoing, but it didn't do any good at all. It was no use. The cop saw me for what I was. He was so sure he knew what I was up to—someone must have been watching out a window—that he slapped the handcuffs on me before I even finished telling him I hadn't done anything wrong.

He shoved me between two abandoned cars parked at the curb, cars that had been stripped of tires and chrome, headlights and windshield wipers—everything that could be stolen off and sold—and within minutes I was standing in front of a surly desk sergeant who was more than ready to lock me up forever for violating my probation. I was charged with malicious mischief this time.

During the days before my trial, everyone tried to tell me I'd get sent to prison, but I didn't believe them. When my case came up at the end of the week, the judge gave me a stern lecture. Then he said, "Miles, I'm going to invoke an active sentence for you. Looks to me like all of a sudden you're trying to head for a life of crime. We'll just see if we can't discourage you a little." I didn't know what he meant to do till he banged his gavel on the heavy oak bench and announced: "Three years in Elmira State Reformatory. Next case."

I was numb.

Chapter V

"Smiley! Look out!"

A black man whirled and sidestepped—just in time. The faceless spread of a heavy gray wool prison blanket was about to be thrown over the inmate's head, pinning his arms to his sides, making him absolutely helpless for whatever beating or knifing or other assault the convicts wanted to lay on him. And he would never know who had done it. He thanked the con whose loud warning had saved him from a brutal beating—or worse.

The con who had cried out was a white man serving time for armed robbery. Somehow he had taken a liking to the black and so had called out to save him, knowing he would have to pay a stiff penalty for it. A prison guard who had seen the whole thing and could have warned the man chose to ignore it completely—temporarily.

The next morning, however, the con who had yelled out the warning was called to the warden's office. We didn't see him for a week after that. When he came back, pale and thin, we didn't have to ask him where he'd been. We knew he'd spent a week in solitary for befriending a black man.

The prison officials did everything they could to discourage friendship between the races. It was my first real encounter with discrimination and prejudice, with hate against the color of a man's skin.

The guards called me "bum'" and "nigger" without any reason that I could see. They treated me in every way as I had heard blacks were treated in the south. White and black were not even permitted to play together in sports, but were kept on opposing teams to keep rivalry stirred up between the races.

There was a great deal of fighting among the inmates. It was easy to get a "white cap," a busted head. And there was gang fighting, just like in the streets. It was a full-time job staying out of trouble, and keeping from having more time added to my sentence.

To protect ourselves against the attacks of other cons, we carried big safety pins and razor blades, stashing them around in places where we could get to them in a hurry.

The old "blanket treatment," unending fighting, homosexual attacks, and hatred of the black man were just a few of the things I learned to watch out for at Elmira. My first few months there were a continual drag of disappointment and frustration, giving me more than my fill of prison life. From the very beginning I determined to follow all the rules to perfection, so I could get out as soon as possible and stay out forever.

It was even in my mind to try to better myself while I was in prison, so I asked to be allowed to finish my schooling. I also wanted training to teach me the trade of tailoring, but I was assigned to duty in the prison laundry instead, although it seemed that everyone else who wanted to go to school or to learn a trade was encouraged and permitted to do so. Why couldn't I be one of them? No one ever explained, and so I began a long stretch of feeling sorry for myself.

I lost my health in the prison laundry, handling heavy loads of steaming clothes and then going outside in the same thin clothes we wore to work in all year round. I was sick half the time, with one cold after another and spells of pneumonia in between.

I was in the prison hospital one day not long after arriving at Elmira and was looking out the window when a riot jumped off in the yard. Once it started, everyone had to be in on it. Pieces of brick flew through the air, and prison shivs usually kept hidden were slashing everywhere, threatening hack and con alike. The hacks worked over more than one rebellious prisoner with their jacks, which were as big as baseball bats and weighted with skull-crushing lead.

The action was finally beginning to get under control when the con who had started it all ran into the tailor shop and came to the door waving a razor-sharp pair of scissors, screaming that he was going to kill someone before it was over. Within seconds the rollers had turned a hose on him and sent the big dogs in to drive him out. He was a pitiful sight when he finally staggered into the yard, his arms crossed protectively over his face, his clothing hanging in bloody shreds where the dogs had torn at him. The dogs were still barking, still lunging at his throat. It made me want to cry. Prison life was not for me. I didn't belong there.

Six months after my release from Elmira I went to Harlem Hospital with TB. They sent me to Otisville Sanatorium where I stayed for nearly a year, thinking I was going to die. When the doctors wanted to operate, to take out some of my ribs and collapse a section of one lung, I wouldn't let them.

"Naw," I said when they tried to get me to sign a paper giving them permission to operate, "if I die, I don't wanna be deformed." I'd seen men after that kind of surgery, all bent over like hunchbacks. "I'm gonna die with all my body I came here with," I said.

But I did get better, in spite of several bouts with pleurisy, and was finally discharged as an arrested tubercular.

People on the outside were very suspicious of anyone who had TB in those days. Although I learned a lot about the disease while I was in the hospital, finding out how to take care of myself, how to explain the disease to other people, and how it wasn't contagious in the way many thought it was, I had a hard time persuading some of my family and friends that it was safe for them to be around me.

There were a few who greeted me affectionately and kissed me, but more who shied away, like I might contaminate them if I got too close. I noticed my sister putting the dishes I ate from on a separate shelf from the others, and if I got a drink of water between meals, she'd stick the glass away where no one else would use it. Some people even seemed to think they would catch TB just from looking at me. I got to the place where I didn't mention my sickness unless someone else brought it up first. I began to believe that everyone was rejecting me. It was frustrating, the feeling that I'd never belong anywhere.

I was so shook up by my first bid in prison, that just as I had tried to be a model prisoner on the inside, so I stayed straight the whole time I was on parole. I did everything right. It would often take a fellow sentenced to a three-year term, five or six years to finish it, because he would be in and out of jail with parole violations so often. But I had had enough of prison. It would never get me again.

I didn't know the devil had something new up his sleeve. But I wasn't long in finding out.

Chapter VI

All at once it was like I could see all hell breaking out in our neighborhood. I don't know where it came from —it just broke out all of a sudden. I heard the guys talking about heroin, the new kick on the street. I didn't start on it myself, just got to hearing about it.

But when it got going pretty strong, I got more and more curious. They say that curiosity killed the cat, and I was about to be that cat.

"What's all this stuff about?" I asked my cousin Robert one day. "I hear you been usin' it, this heroin stuff. You a big wheel anyway. Tell me what's goin' on."

"Man, it's cool!" he told me, acting glad I'd asked

him and rolling his eyes up to the top of his head like it was really something wonderful.

"Ya kin git high on just takin' a snort, man," he told me, "just sniffin' it up yore nose. Ummm—mellow, man! One little whiff and ya feel just great! Ya don't throw up, no hangover, no nuthin'—just a good ole high, high, high—"

"Don't soun' like it'd hurt me none just to try some," I decided, thinking it over. "Got any?" I asked, digging in my pocket for some money.

"Yeah, man," he said, shoving my arm aside so I couldn't reach my money. "An' ya don't need to pay me fer this first one—this one's on me, man!" He was peddling caps in those days, for just a dollar a cap, enough heroin to keep you high all day.

I'll never forget how I felt when I took that first snort, what they call blowing through your nose. Three or four of us were standing in the dark littered corner of the stairway of a ghetto apartment, where it turned to go up another flight. We could hear the sounds of radios, of fighting and cursing in some of the nearby apartments, and as usual, the smell in the air was enough to knock you out. Little kids coming home from school crowded past us, saying, "Please let me by, Mister," not even curious about what we were up to, they had seen everything so many times.

Robert showed me how to sniff the white powder, pouring it from the little plastic capsule into a folded matchbook cover and holding it close to my nose. I tried it, just like he showed me, being careful not to spill any of it.

Nothing much happened at first, except a kind of good feeling, like a warm blanket being pulled over you on a cold night. Robert went on about his business, and I shrugged my shoulders and headed for my girl's house, several blocks away.

The next thing I knew, I was coming to, opening my eyes to find myself lying in a stairwell where I had fallen, halfway on one step and halfway on another. My back was painfully bruised. I tested my legs to see if there were any broken bones.

When I could sit up, I spread my legs to get them out of the way and heaved all the insides of my stomach onto the bumpy steel treads of the gritty steps below me. The sour acid smell drowned out all the other stench of the ghetto for a few moments; then all the usual smells blended together again as if nothing new had been added.

I wiped my face on my shirttail and staggered outside for some better air. I could tell I was going to be all right.

All right? Man, I was more than all right! I felt it as soon as I got in the sun—warm peace just flooded over me, like it was being poured out of a big honey pitcher in the sky, and I was standing under it, soaking all of it up—all for me. All my troubles were gone, and everything in the world belonged to me, and I belonged to it, too. If this was what heroin did, I could see why everybody wanted to start using it. I could have floated to the moon if I'd wanted to. Man! But I didn't want to go anywhere else—I'd have been content to stay forever, just feeling the peace pouring over me right there on the sidewalk. Sniffing my high didn't make me sick again, but I'd have stayed with it even if it did, it was that wonderful.

Two weeks later I was standing in the alley behind my place, snorting a high, when some of my friends came along.

"Man," Danny said, grinning at me, "you shore is wastin' yore money."

"How come?" I wanted to know, waiting for my high to hit me. Because I was on welfare, still recovering from TB and not supposed to go to work yet, the cost of the drug hadn't bothered me, but I wondered what he meant.

"Snortin's too slow, fer one thing," he said, and the others nodded their heads in vigorous agreement. "Ya don't wanna be snortin' it ferever—that was just ta git ya started. Snortin's a waste of drugs. Come on, man, time ta git with it. Take the needle, take the needle!"

The next day I watched my friends take the needle in a shooting gallery up in the top of an apartment building where nobody lived anymore. The windows were all broken out, the doors boarded up, and rats were so thick you could step on them, even in the daytime.

The guys took off their belts and looped them around their arms until the veins bulged out thick and heavy. Then they stuck their needles in and the blood started running down, scaring me so bad I knew I'd have to take the needle too, to prove I was brave enough to belong.

One of the guys could see I wasn't too keen on it.

"Ya kin take a skin pop if ya don't wanna mainline," he said. "That's still better'n snortin' it."

But I couldn't let them see I was scared.

"Come off it, man," I told them, unbuckling my belt and trying to keep my hands from shaking. "Don'tcha know all that time I been in the hospital with the TB? I had so many needles in me there, for fluid tappin' 'n' such, that I don't think nuthin' of it. Fact of the matter, I don't feel 'xactly right *without* a needle in me," I lied. I could feel my voice quavering at the thought of it.

"Here, lemme have the needle and I'll show ya," I bragged. Danny handed me his works, and I rinsed it out in the water we'd collected from a rain puddle on the roof, water already pinkish from having everybody else rinse his bloody needle in it.

Danny poured part of a cap of dope into an old spoon, added some clear rain water, held a match under it for a few seconds, and then drew it up into the needle for me. I took a deep breath, jabbed it hard and deep into my vein, and pushed the plunger of the hypo.

The beautiful warm glow spread over me immediately, inside and outside, every inch of me alive to it, melting me down, like spilled ice cream on a hot sidewalk. Man, it was wonderful! Better'n havin' a woman. An' right now! An' it didn't quit, just kep' on glowin' and spreadin' over and over and over.

I couldn't have known that the wonderfulness was the beginning of nineteen years of hell.

Chapter VII

"Yeah? Whatcha want?"

A skinny black waitress in a thin white uniform flounced up to my table in the gritty little restaurant. I pretended to study the menu, smudged with greasy fingerprints and spilled ketchup. Actually, I was keeping my mind on the two cops across the street, cops who seemed to be watching the door of the restaurant where I was supposed to be making the biggest drug pickup of my life. I had never been more scared, more unsure of what I ought to do. I wanted to run—to make a break for it—but that could be the end of me.

The waitress stood impatiently first on one foot and then on the other, waiting for my order.

"I ain't got all day," she whined. I wondered why not—there were only four other customers in the place, and they had already been served sauerkraut and hot dogs. The stinking odor along with the filthiness of the place made me feel nauseated.

"Just coffee," I said finally, plunking a dime down on the table.

"Black or with?" she snapped, putting the money in her pocket.

"Black," I barked back at her.

She jabbed her pencil at a blank on her order pad and swung back to the serving station, returning with a not quite clean heavy white cup and saucer in one hand and a battered aluminum coffeepot in the other. Clattering the cup and saucer down in front of me, she poured the coffee too fast, making it slosh out into the saucer, leaving the cup only half full when she finished. I drew back to keep from being spattered myself. She didn't apologize, just muttered an indignant "Hmph!" and disappeared into the kitchen.

My mind didn't linger on her disposition or the filth around me or the sickening smell of the food, however. I emptied the saucer into the coffee cup and gulped the lukewarm brew to try to take the chill of fear away from me.

The connection man had told me I'd find the package of dope in the top of the paper towel cabinet in the men's room of the restaurant. That fact floated on top of my mind. It was awash with fear. *Do the cops already know about it?* I wondered. *Are they waiting to catch me redhanded? If I leave without getting the stuff, the pusher will kill me!*

Cold sweat broke out on my forehead as I shoved my chair back and started to get out of it to go to the men's room. But one of the other men in the place got up ahead of me, a big ugly fellow with a jagged scar on his cheek. *Is he here to keep me in line?* I shuddered at the thought of it, easing back into my chair to wait.

When he opened the door and came out of the men's room, buckling his belt, I could hear the protesting whine of a flushed toilet and a "glug, glug" that told me it was in working order. *Maybe that's the answer! I can dispose of the stuff down the toilet and save myself from the law and the pusher. I can go out clean and pretend that the stuff was already gone when I arrived.*

But my nose was already beginning to be sniffly, a sure sign that I was going to need my shot soon myself. Besides, I had a sinking feeling that the pusher would hold me responsible no matter what happened. I began to hope fervently that I would find the stuff exactly where it was supposed to be.

Going into the tiny bathroom with its warped green asbestos tile floor and the flaking paint on its dirt-splotched walls, I wondered how the brutish giant of a man had been able to close the door behind him. There was barely room for me. I turned to hook the screen-door type lock behind me and looked around. The rusting paper-towel holder was attached to the wall above a grimy pockmarked sink. The holder was the kind you open from the front with a key when you want to put more towels in.

A key! Minnie forgot to give me a key! I couldn't get to the stuff without a key unless I tore the box off the wall and caused a lot of commotion. I knew Minnie wouldn't like that.

I felt under the lining of my shoe for a tiny scrap of paper with Minnie's telephone number on it. I'd have to risk a call.

"Now don't you let nuthin' go wrong, Floyd boy," he'd told me. " 'Cause iffen you do—" He made a funny noise in his throat as he drew his finger across the front of his neck like he was slashing somebody's head off—mine. I knew he meant I'd be a dead pigeon —all gone—if I didn't come through for him.

The telephone was in a bright red booth in the front left corner of the restaurant. I was grateful that it was enclosed so I could shut the door, and I just had to trust that it wasn't bugged. My hand shook as I dialed the number.

When a voice that sounded deliberately calm answered, "Yes?" I said, "It's me. I can't do nuthin'. Ya din't give me a key." I exhaled, relieved that I couldn't get to the stuff, glad it wasn't my fault.

"A key? Why, you—! Whadja need a key fer? Just git the stuff and hurry on back." Minnie wasn't noted for his patience.

"But that's just it—" I argued. "I can't git the stuff without ya give me a key to open where it's at."

"Dumhead!" he shouted. "Ya don't need no key! That lock is just fer show. Ya open the thing from the top, from the back of the top, stupid. Go try it. And git the hell back here. We got customers waitin'!"

I had seen the customers on my way to the restaurant—all up and down Eighth Avenue, standing in doorways and on streetcorners, waiting for someone to deliver the stuff for a fix before they got sicker than they were already. Ragged, bleary-eyed, grizzled, wobbly, toothless, snotty-nosed derelicts of humanity. I wondered how long it would take before I looked like that. Addicts didn't stay young long. And I was as hooked as they were, just better able to support my habit because I was strong enough to hustle.

"Ya *still* there?" The voice at the other end of the telephone sounded like it would explode any minute.

"Yeah, I'm still here," I admitted.

"Well, git movin'—" The voice was menacing, like a final warning. I could imagine Minnie gritting his teeth at me.

"There's another problem," I explained, watching the cops through the glass side of the phone booth. "Couple of bulls across the street watchin' this place like it was about to git away—"

"Ohhh!" he groaned, like he was holding his head in his hands. "Why'd I have to pick such a *baby* fer this job? Don'tcha know *nuthin'* yet? Them bulls is on the payroll, same as you. They're gonna make sure nobody interferes with yore bizness, that's all. Now, man, *git movin'.*" He slammed the receiver down, nearly busting my eardrum.

I'd run into crooked cops before, but never even dreamed of anything like that! Cops actually running interference for pushers? It was hard to believe. But I had to trust Minnie to know what he was talking about.

I shoved the door of the phone booth to the side and strolled back to the men's room, casual like, patting my coat pockets and trying to look puzzled as if I'd forgotten something and was going back to look for it. The lid of the towel cabinet lifted easy, just like Minnie said it would, and I pulled out a brown paper bag loaded with stuff, the most I'd ever seen in one bunch in my life! At first I thought I had hold of a bag of soap or something, it was that heavy. There were ten packs or pieces of stuff, ten ounces, probably worth close to six thousand dollars on the street. It was too big for me to try to hide it under my jacket, so I just carried the bag out in the open, in the crook of my arm in full view, like I was taking home a bag of donuts or something. I walked deliberately slow, though I wanted to run, holding my breath till I got to the sidewalk. I felt as conspicuous as a Santa Claus in July.

I let pass the first cab that came along, afraid it might be planted, and got the second one, switching from one cab to another three times on the way to Minnie's, so I could shake whoever might be following me.

After I delivered the stuff, got to my place and locked the door behind me, I sat down and shook for half an hour. It sure had looked like I was being set up there for a while. But now I had enough stuff in my pocket to last for several days. I could take a vacation, just stay in and goof off.

I hadn't wanted to get involved in dealing dope—too risky—and at first I hadn't needed to. When my welfare check came in every month I was able to buy a good supply of stuff. But after a while, as my habit grew, the welfare check wasn't big enough to buy all the dope my habit called for. And I had to become a professional thief—stealing, hustling, breaking into cars and stores—as a full-time occupation. Gradually I became sharper, keener, knew what to look out for and how to grab it. Later, when even that didn't provide enough money, I had to go big-time, and get mixed up in dealing dope.

The first time I broke into a car, I threw a brick through the side window. Turk was with me that day. I was trying to show him how to support his habit without sponging off his mother and his girl friends all the time. I didn't know then that there were better ways of getting into a car than breaking windows. It was Sonny Stump who showed me a better way one day. And before long, I could open a locked car door with a piece of coat-hanger wire faster than a garage-man could get into one with a key.

But on that particular day, Turk and his brother were with me when I spotted a light tan gabardine overcoat on the front seat of a car parked near Amsterdam and Columbia. They stood a little ways off while I broke the window and opened the door to grab the coat. There were other people in the neighborhood, but no one paid any particular attention to what I was up to. I put the coat on, and my friends walked with me to the pawnshop five or six blocks away. There I took the coat off and shoved it under the heavy iron gratings that stretched from the counter to the ceiling.

"Yes?" the white pawnshop man said, hardly looking at me over his steel-rimmed glasses.

"Gimme twenty," I said.

He looked the coat over—the label, the buttonholes, the lining, the sleeves—and held it up to make sure it was in good condition.

"Ten," he countered.

"Aw," I cried. "It's a *good* coat. Make it fifteen?" He shrugged his shoulders and pushed a form across the counter at me. With the stub of a yellow pencil tied to the grating with a dirty string, I wrote down a made-up name, Richard Wilson, and a nearby address. The man transferred the information to a ticket, tore it in two, handed me part of it and tucked the other part in the pocket of the coat. Turk and his brother and I walked out, no questions asked.

"See how easy it is?" I boasted. "Absolutely nuthin' to it." We went on to a pusher, bought enough dope to share, and then bought hot dogs and candy with the money that was left.

Sometimes, instead of taking stolen goods to the pawnshop, I went directly to the consumer. I walked down to the garment district where workers were pushing open trucks of dresses—some in boxes, some on racks—down the streets. I copped a few off the back of a truck and had them sold before anyone knew they were gone. It was a cinch to sell any kind of hot merchandise in Harlem, because everyone was always looking for a bargain. I went into apartment houses and knocked on any door. When someone called out, "Who's there?" I answered, "Would you like to buy a nice dress, Miss? I got some beautiful sample dresses here to sell." If she was scared she'd say, "No, thanks," but they generally let me in. I opened the boxes and held up the dresses, told them what the sizes were, and named my price.

When someone asked, "Can I try it on?" I acted like they had committed a crime.

"Try it on? No good! This ain't no store. Ya might tear somethin'. Buy it as is—"

I started folding the dresses back into the box, and sometimes they bought something then—in a hurry and at my price. But sometimes they tried to jew me down, and make it not worthwhile stealing it to start with.

"Whadya mean, it didn't cost me nuthin'?" I accused them indignantly. "Why, I'm risking the pen every time I bring you somethin'—if I got caught, you wouldn't see me for a year!" Sometimes that would help them see that I deserved a little something for my trouble.

Customers ordered things from me, just like I was a store or a mail-order house. They described a style they wanted, and I looked around and tried to steal it for them, the right color, the right size even. They were happy to buy it—sometimes for more than it would have cost them in a store.

One night I was strolling through the garment center, not hurting for a fix yet, but keeping my eyes open for something big that would be worth my trouble. I spotted a salesman's car. The back seat was piled high with brown traveling boxes, the kind that would have five or six dresses or suits in each one. It looked like a perfect opportunity to make a good clean haul, clear several hundred dollars without half trying. There were people around, but it was a white neighborhood and there wasn't a bull in sight as far as I could see. Generally, if there wasn't a cop on the spot, the whites wouldn't pay any attention to a black getting into something. I was a good short cracker by then, and it was the work of just a few seconds to get the car unlocked with a stolen screwdriver I happened to have on me—just in case of a golden opportunity. As soon as the screwdriver had done its job, I threw it as far as I could. I always did that, ever since the time I got charged with possession of "burglar tools" when a bull found a screwdriver in my pocket.

I opened the back door and began unloading boxes

onto the sidewalk. If anyone had come along to question me, I'd have made like the merchandise was mine and I was a salesman making a general delivery. There'd be no sign the car had been tampered with, and I wouldn't have anything suspicious on my person.

"Freeze!"

I was half inside the car, in the middle of removing a fifth box to add to the pile I already had on the sidewalk when a voice rang out from across the street. I was so startled, I dropped the box in my hand and caught my breath. Through the car window I could see a man with a snub-nosed .38 in his hand. He was more than ready for whatever foolishness I might think of trying. There wasn't going to be any foolishness as far as I was concerned, not under those circumstances. I knew better than to try to run from bullets. Although he wasn't in uniform, I knew instinctively that the white man was a cop. I could smell one out a mile away, with kind of a sixth sense I'd developed about the police. I could spot them every time. Seemed like the white cops I could tell because they didn't have any fear of the black man, and the black ones, well, they'd start closing in, getting too close for no reason at all.

Backing slowly out of the car, I stood with my hands stretched high over my head and waited while he patted me down and put the handcuffs on, locking my hands behind my back. He checked out the title certificate in the glove compartment of the salesman's car and then steered me through the crowd that had come out of a bar to see the excitement. We crossed the street to where his car was parked. He opened the door for me to get in the back seat, pushed the lock button down, and walked around to the front. The crowd was slowly straggling back inside the bar as we pulled away from the curb and headed for the precinct.

I figured that someone must have seen me, someone who went into a bar and maybe told the bartender that a black man was taking things out of a car across the street. The bartender wouldn't have been interested, but this off-duty detective must have overheard the conversation. He *was* interested.

I was crying for mercy, trying to get out of being booked, dreading the withdrawal agonies I'd face if he didn't let me go.

"Give me somebody," he offered finally, "somebody bigger'n you."

"I don't know nobody—nobody but dope fiends," I said, knowing he'd have to have a pusher, somebody big-time before he'd let me go.

"Well, then, ya got any money?" he asked.

"Naw," I said. "What would I be doing this for if I had anything? Can't ya just take the merchandise?" Plenty of cops did, I knew.

But he shook his head.

"Is there anybody who'll give me some money for ya?" he wanted to know.

"Yeah," I answered eagerly. "I can get some from my fence—if you'll let me go to him."

"Not a chance," he barked. "You tell me where to find him and *I'll* go."

"I can't do that," I said at first, out of some kind of loyalty to the code of honor among thieves.

But I didn't particularly like my fence, and I gave in after the detective promised to book me on a jive beef, a petty larceny charge, instead of what I was really guilty of.

"Well, go up and see my friend Bob," I said. "He lives uptown." I gave him the address. "Tell him I sent you."

At the precinct he threw the book at me, really put me in the cross. I'd never been double-crossed so bad. And I learned later that he shook Bob down for several hundred dollars.

When I got to thinking straight, I could see that I should have kept my mouth shut from the very beginning. I should have known he couldn't let me off easy—too many people had seen the whole thing. He'd have been getting himself in trouble if he had done me any favors.

I kept on stealing everywhere I could, even though there was always some risk. Addicts had no choice. We'd have been glad to steal a gold tooth out of a dead man's mouth, just to buy a fix. If there was an accident, we raced to see who could get to it first. Someone's pocketbook, or billfold, or wristwatch might have fallen to the street. And the crowd was always fair game for purse snatching.

I stole from my family, too. I went to my mother's

apartment when I knew she was away and took a toaster, a radio, a pair of shoes, my stepfather's suit, a blanket—anything worth a dollar—and took it to a pawnshop for some quick money. I always meant to get it back for them as soon as I had made a quick sting, a big haul, but somehow I never got around to it. The family finally told me I had to get out, and they changed the locks on their doors so I couldn't steal them blind.

I wasn't even above stealing from my own children when I saw them on the streets. One day my little boy came up to me with some pennies and nickels in his pocket that his great-grandmother had given him to buy a loaf of bread from the store on the corner.

"Let daddy hold yer money fer ya a minute," I said. Then I got his mind off on something else and made him forget his money so I could keep it. I'd even take my son and daughter around to visit aunts or cousins, hoping they would give the kids a dollar or two that I could get away from them. It took all I could scrape together to support my habit. I couldn't afford to care who I hurt.

My mother had gotten me out on bail one time when I was expecting to go up for trial in a few days and get a suspended sentence. My lawyer had almost promised me that I'd get off easy. I was dealing dope at the time and had some at the house, about two-dozen five-dollar bags of it. There was money too, two or three thousand dollars that I owed my connection man. I put it all, heroin and money together, into a big brown envelope and handed it to my mother, on the outside chance that I might get some time after all.

"Keep this fer me, Mom, while I go down to be tried today," I told her, not saying what was in the bag. "I know the judge is gonna let me off with a suspended sentence, but in case I don't come back, give this here to Scopes—he'll be comin' by fer it." She knew Scopes because he had grown up in our neighborhood, but she wanted to know more about it.

"What's in the bag?" she asked me, sounding a little suspicious.

"Don't worry about that," I said, impatient with her. "Just give it to him." She finally agreed.

Turned out the judge put me away for six months, but I was so high when I walked into the jail that I didn't even care. It hit me a few hours later—hard. Man!

By the next week, Scopes hadn't showed up at the house and Mom didn't know how to get in touch with him. She got to worrying, nervous about what might be in the bag, and thought she'd better take a look. When she saw the bags of white powdery stuff, she started flushing them down the toilet as fast as she could. The next visiting day, I was in the hospital, but she really laid me out.

"I should've dumped the money down along with it," she said. I almost jumped out of the bed.

"Bunky," she went on, "don'tcha have any decency —any care at all what that dope makes ya do to people? Yer own mother—what if a cop had come to the house and found all that stuff there in my bedroom? Why, I'd 'a' been put in jail too!" She shook her head at me and sniffed, not able to understand how her own son could be as low as all that.

I shrugged, not caring about the hell of worry I put her through all the time. I was just dreaming of the day when I'd get out so I could get high again. It got so bad that she was glad to see me in prison. And she wasn't afraid to tell me so.

"Oh, Bunky, ya look so good when ya git in jail, all cleaned up 'n' some meat on yer bones. I don't hafta think of ya out in the streets, dead from a cop's bullet or a OD or from some gang kid knifin' ya." She stopped long enough to fish a handkerchief from the folds of her sleeve. "If ya only could come home after this stretch 'n' start over agin 'n' do right—git yerself a job 'n'—"

"Yeah, Mama, yeah, okay," I said, wishing she would leave. "Only don't cry, Mama." Her tears were making me nervous. I knew down deep that the only starting over I would do would be in the wrong direction, starting over again on dope. I licked my lips, thinking about how wonderful that first high was going to be—

When I was in jail, I almost forgot about the rat race of running the stuff down and getting enough scratch to pay for it. But on the outside, my mind was active day and night; even in my sleep, my subconscious had to be scheming, mapping out plans for getting that next shot. I couldn't really rest unless I knew where the next fix was coming from. It was that desperate with me.

Sometimes I woke up with my nose running, the hard cramps beginning in my stomach, and I was so tired, so beat, that I prayed, "Oh, God, please let me stay in, just this one time. I don't feel like shootin' no dope." I dozed off again for a little while and woke up sicker than before. "I don't feel like gittin' out and stealin' nuthin'," I groaned, but He never answered those prayers.

I looked around the house to see what I could take to the pawnshop. And then I decided, "No, I don't wanna steal nuthin' from the house," and I had to get up and go out on the street. I tried to cop the first thing I saw, maybe break into a car just for an umbrella to hock. There were people walking up and down, but I was too sick to care who saw me.

If I happened to have a girl friend who could go out and sell herself for me, then sometimes I just sacked in with my misery, just laid there in the crib waiting for her to come back. And if she took very long, I got impatient, wondering whether she'd ever come back or not. The longer I was an addict, the more impatient I became. That was a definite handicap to me. Some of the guys could make lots of money with very little risk, being con artists, conning people out of something. But that took patience, and I was no good at it. I felt too much like knocking a guy in the head and grabbing whatever he had and running with it.

And sometimes there were dope panics when nobody could get any stuff, even if they had the bread for it. It would happen when the police got really hot on the trail of the pushers, and they'd have to go underground and stay a week or two until things cooled off.

The price of dope would go up from five to maybe thirty dollars a bag, and there'd be more "dummies"—bags with lye, soap powder, baking powder, and such—than real stuff on the market.

Addicts would be waiting, waiting, waiting, on street corners, swallowing bottle after bottle of wine, trying to survive until some stuff came around. They'd be sniffly, vomiting all over themselves, doubled over with the cramps of withdrawal, craving a fix.

One Saturday morning in the midst of a panic, a pusher showed up with a shopping bag on the corner by the candy store. He was keeping careful lookout in every direction, not wanting to risk having the man come down on him.

"Okay, I got it," he said, when he thought the coast was clear. "There's enough for everybody—only make it snappy. If ya wanna cop some dope from me, have yer money ready—fifteen dollars a bag today—and I don't want one penny short."

The addicts fell all over themselves—and each other—crowding in for one of the precious bags of life. Somebody opened a bag and stuck a wet finger down inside, to make sure he was getting the real thing. When he put the familiar bitterness to his tongue, he grinned sickly from ear to ear and scrambled up the stairs to the rooftop where he had his works hidden.

A few minutes later, while the sidewalk was still jammed with derelicts waiting to cop their dope, the fellow who had tasted his bag leaned his head over the edge of the roof and screamed to the crowd below, "Kill him! Kill him! It's a lemon! It's a lemon!" He paused for breath and went on, his voice growing more and more shrill. "He's burnin' ya! He's burnin' ya!"

The pusher, who had put quinine,* not heroin, in the bags, threw the rest of the worthless bags high into the air. Addicts who hadn't understood the conversation from the rooftop scrambled after the bags which were strewn all over the sidewalk. The pusher jumped into his car and zoomed off down the street, leaving a pitifully sick and angry mob staring helplessly after him.

I wasn't in the panic, just heard about it later after some of the guys who got burned went to the pusher's apartment and methodically broke his arms and legs.

We addicts lived in an up and down world. We couldn't depend on anything or anybody, but when the dope was good, that was enough to make up for everything.

In nineteen years I was arrested and convicted

* Quinine, being bitter, passed the taste test, but it didn't produce a high when the man shot it in his vein.

thirty or forty times. I wound up serving ten or twelve years in jail—on the installment plan.

Every time I was caught, I had to go through the hell of kicking my habit cold turkey in jail. I did it so often I could predict how long it would take me and how I'd feel.

Generally I was in a cell with another guy, and the withdrawals wouldn't hit me real bad until I was locked up a few hours, depending on how long ago I took off. It started with me feeling kind of bad, yawning, sniffing like I had a bad head cold starting up. Then the cramps hit my stomach, pain that nearly tore my guts out; and the vomiting that kept on long after my insides were stripped bare; and then the diarrhea that wouldn't quit, that sent me running every two minutes for fear I wouldn't make it in time. Finally I got so weak that I didn't even bother to try to make it to the toilet but lay in my own filth and didn't even care.

At the Tombs there were springs on the beds in the cells, but no mattresses. Prisoners were given three or four blankets. We folded three of them up to lie on and kept the other one for a cover over us. Often I got sick and vomited all over myself.

"Officer," I called to the roller, or, if I knew his name, "Mr. Gregory."

"Yeah, whadya want?" the hack yelled back at me.

"I vomited all over my blanket," I said.

"Well, whadya want *me* to do about it?" Some of

the rollers were like that, always trying to make it hard on us.

"Could I have a clean blanket, please?"

Some told me to wait until the boy who took care of things like that came back on the floor, and then I could change the messed-up blanket for a clean one. Others weren't so kind.

"Now, ain't that a pity," they jeered. "Ya puked on yerself and now ya don't like it—that's tough." Then I tried to wash the blanket the best I could in the cold water in the toilet bowl. Our sinks were too small for us to do much washing in them.

Some of the hacks really put us through the changes, turning off the radio when they came on duty so we didn't have anything to listen to, throwing us under icy cold showers for no reason, and beating us unmercifully for the least little thing. Many times I heard of an inmate being treated so bad that he had to go to the hospital. Word would get out that he got pneumonia and died from that, but we knew what it was that killed him.

One of the doctors was known as "the butcher" because so many cons died under his knife, almost as if he was trying to get rid of them. One of my friends was making a good recovery from TB and a serious cardiac condition when he developed a urinary infection and couldn't pass his water. "Money," as we used to call him, was always a good hustler, and the operation to relieve his trouble was supposed to be a minor one, just routine surgery. When he came up from under the knife, they buried him. We were all mad as hell about it, thinking it wouldn't have happened if the doctor had really cared.

Often patients would be given massive shots of morphine for pain, and we'd never see them again.

There were some easygoing guards too, who tried to show us some kindness. They pretended not to notice when some of us had some swag, some contraband, like leftover food smuggled out of the kitchen. We laid a cold pork chop on our steel bunk or set a tin cup of coffee there and made a torch out of a roll of toilet paper, set a match to it, and held it under the bunk until the chop was warmed or the coffee was steaming hot.

The "good rollers" turned their heads the other way if they thought we were stealing sugar from the officers' mess. We called this swagging of food, "jailhouse juggling." The extra sugar was especially important to addicts. We ate it like candy, and it would help to satisfy the gnawing craving in our guts. The craving never stopped.

Time after time I staggered around the familiar cells, tripping over my bunk, my cellmate, my own unmanageable feet, and even the floor, trying to find some position I could stand, some way I could get away from myself. I was too weak to sleep, too weak to eat to regain my strength, and I had to spend my pitiful supply of energy in trying not to scream. If I yelled too loud, I was likely to get a club laid up by the side of my head. Sometimes I would even welcome that—it would take my mind from my other miseries.

On top of all that, I got sick with the TB again. I was in Sing Sing when I became critically ill with a fever of 106°. Because they had no arrangement to treat TB there, I was transferred to the hospital at Dannemore State Prison where they could give me the help I needed. But the doctors were not very encouraging about my case. I arrived shackled to a sheriff and was put immediately into an emergency room where they expected me to die. I didn't know why they had bothered with the handcuffs—I was too sick to think about going anywhere, except maybe to hell. But there was a new doctor there—from Germany—and he had new medicines like streptomycin and penicillin, so instead of dying I started getting better.

And soon I was back on the streets. But I never stayed there long. I was back in jail, over and over again.

Sometimes, in thirty days, or sixty, or ninety—whenever my time was up and I was released from prison—I decided to take just one more shot, for old time's sake, one last shot and be through with dope forever.

It happened to some guys just that way, only not like I was thinking.

One day, along about October, I was walking down the street feeling great. The weather was the kind I loved, lots of blue in the sky and puffy clouds floating around, a little breeze, and a warm lazy feel to the air.

I had just finished a six-months' stretch and was in perfect health. I was back on dope again, but it hadn't really got to me yet.

From a distance down the block I recognized Snuffy sitting on the steps of his apartment. He'd been doing a stretch for larceny, too, and had just gotten home that very day. Man, was I glad to see him!

"Hey, Snuffy!" I yelled, and several guys in the area turned to look, but Snuffy didn't budge. He just sat there, staring straight ahead. I knew he was nuttin' on me, pretending not to hear me.

"Hey, Snuff old man, ya can't fool me," I teased.

I had walked up close enough by then to see that his pockets had been turned inside out. I thought he was sleeping and that somebody had rolled him.

"Hey, straighten up there, man," I yelled at him. "What's wrong with you?" I gave him a playful punch on the arm. When I did, he tilted over and bumped off the side of the steps, landing on the concrete sidewalk with a dull thud, his eyes still looking straight ahead, his knees bent like they were when he was sitting down. He'd been dead with an OD long enough for rigor mortis to set in.

A puppy that had scooted off when I came up crept back, licking Snuffy's face and kind of whimpering at him. I didn't dare be caught on the scene, but I was glad for the pup. His whimpering sounded like the sadness, the pity, I felt inside. But I couldn't stay with Snuffy, no matter how sorry I felt.

The police might think I had given him an OD myself and book me for homicide. I might be able to beat the rap, but I didn't want to be held for questioning because I wouldn't get to shoot up on time and would have to go through being sick.

I ran two blocks before I dared to stop and knock at a door.

"Dead man down the street!" I shouted at the man who came to the door. I didn't stop to explain anything, just pointed in the direction from which I had come. Then I got in the wind and took off, trusting he'd call the police. It was too late for the doctor. When I got out of the neighborhood, I sat down on some steps and cried my heart out. Snuffy had had his one last shot.

But there was no such thing as a last shot for me. Every time I got out of jail, I had to go right back into stealing to support a brand-new habit, worse than the old one had ever been. I was getting my OD the slow way. Only I just couldn't die.

It was like drugs made up for the happiness and love I was missing in my life. They made me forget that I was a failure, that I didn't belong to anybody, and that nobody belonged to me. I gave up everything—and everybody—for drugs. My wife, my children, my mother—

Life was a vicious circle of prison and drugs, drugs and prison.

I came before one judge, Judge Hoffman his name was, so often that he usually asked me, "How much time should I give you this trip, young man?" Everybody loved Judge Hoffman. Another judge, Judge Bresley, told me if I would put as much effort into being a good citizen as I put into being a worthless drug addict, I'd probably get to be president some day.

I was in and out of jail so much that I became "institutionalized" and felt more at home *in* jail than out of it. Among the living dead as I called them, I was a perfectly good citizen. I had a chance there to be clean, and healthy, and think about something besides how to get that next shot. And I made great resolutions in jail. We all did.

"Ah, man, I'm cuttin' that dope a-loose," we promised each other.

But the outside world kept coming in, along with the new prisoners from the streets, and we couldn't help asking about it.

"What's happening out there?" we wanted to know. "Who got killed? Who's got the good dope? Who took an OD?" And we began to think about being in the exciting swing of things again ourselves, forgetting the parts that hurt. Our good resolutions in jail never lasted long enough to help us on the outside.

Once in a while, I'd think a little higher. After my wife died, especially, I started to read serious books to see if I could find the answer to my problems. I read books on religion, on psychology, on black people.

Psychiatrists and social workers in the prisons tried to reach us. "Why do you use drugs?" they asked. We couldn't tell them the answers, because we didn't know them ourselves. Sometimes they praised us to the skies: "You seem like such a good man—you have such potential. You shouldn't be living like this." We knew they were right, but the knowledge just drove us further and further into our guilt. They didn't have any answers for us, only questions and more questions.

There were people on the outside who wanted to help us, too. My sister, who often arranged bail for me and let me stay at her place when I had nowhere else to go, begged me to stop doping and shape up and live right. The rest of the family did the same thing, but none of them ever had any real confidence in me, not enough to hand me some money and tell me to go buy some clothes and get myself a job. They never followed up on seeing that I got started straight. They left it up to me, wishing me well. And I wasn't strong enough to make it on my own. I headed for the pusher, for comfort from the needle.

Finally I got so low I wouldn't even go see my own people. I couldn't blame them for being ashamed of me, but I didn't like to look at it in their eyes. And so, ragged and dirty, I slept in damp cellars, in basements where the rats ran over me, in hallways cluttered with filth, and in winter I even rode the subways all night trying to keep warm.

Sometimes I woke up to find my legs swollen so bad from the blood not circulating in them that I couldn't straighten them. The pain nearly made me pass out. I didn't have lice like the winos did, but the filth of my body and my body odor was so bad I could hardly stand it.

I used that for an excuse to go to my sister and ask for money to buy a new shirt and take a bath. She gave it to me, and I always spent it on dope and then stole a shirt and took a bath at a friend's house so she'd think I'd spent the money like I promised.

I figured I would die before long. It couldn't happen too soon to suit me.

One day a prison psychologist was giving me one of their regular tests. He asked me to draw four pictures for him—a house, a man, a woman, and a tree.

"Now, Miles," he said, when I had completed them, "if you were to die and come back to life, which one of these would you like to come back as—a house, a man, a woman, or a tree?"

"Come back as?" I laughed in his face. "I wouldn't wanna come back as nuthin'. I'd wanna stay dead. I can't hardly wait to get that way."

And I meant every word of it.

Chapter VIII

I was tired. Sick to the heart of me. Bone-weary of the lying, the cheating, the stealing, the needle, the prison, the shame, the agony of kicking my habit cold turkey over and over again only to head for a pusher the first thing when I was back on the street. I was ready to try anything for relief. *Is this gonna be the rest of my life, in and out of prison, off and on dope?* I wondered. It didn't seem worth sticking around for—

One day Phil and I—he was an addict like me—pooled our money and bought a five-dollar bag of dope. We went to the rooftop to shoot up together, both of us hungry and ragged, and after we got high I said to him, "Come on, man, let's go git us somethin' to eat. Let's go to that store there—," I pointed to a big supermarket at the end of the block, "and cop us some cans and fill our stomachs." Phil looked at me for a long minute and shook his head, his loose jowls flopping against his shirt collar.

"Naw," he said, "Let's not do it thataway. I know a place down the street where we can eat good—a hot meal—free, and no risk."

"Yer kiddin'," I told him, looking into his bleary bloodshot eyes. "I never heard tell of no place like that, and I've lived here near 'bout all my life. Whatcha talkin' 'bout?"

"Well, it's kind of a church," he said apologetically, wiping his nose on the raveled-out sleeve of his dirty blue sweater. "On 124th Street. Called a soul-saving station or somethin' like that. They feed folks there every day—addicts and winos and all kinda strays from the street—like us," he grinned.

"Yeah?" I found it hard to believe. "I've prob'ly passed it a million times then without seein' it—" I said. But I got up from where I had been sitting, leaned against the soot-stained chimney. "Come on, man. I'm game. Let's go on down there."

"But ya gotta lissen to the preachin' first—before they feed ya," he warned, two missing teeth in the front of his mouth making his voice whistle.

"Well, I guess I can take that if you can," I sighed. "How long does the preachin' last?" I knotted the rope that held my pants up and felt of the stubble of beard on my face.

He scratched his head for a minute and examined

his fingernails before he answered. "Well, the preachin' don't last *too* long, and they serve some mighty nice meals."

We headed down the stairway, the holey soles of our shoes flopping on every step. We shuffled in silence the two or three blocks to the church. Sure enough, there it was, looking like all the other brownstones except for a neat black and white sign hung on the front: "Soul-saving station."

I shoved the door open and saw thirty or forty people sitting on folding chairs inside—boys, girls, wineheads, dopeheads, homos, and even a few squares. Some were well-dressed—looked like they could afford to buy the place. But most looked like I knew I must look—as if without their ragged clothes to hold them together they'd fall apart completely.

Man, I thought when we lined up for food, *they sure won't need no garbage cans here, because there won't be no leftovers left over—not if everybody's as hungry as I am!*

They really fed us that day, too. Sitting down to the hot, rich, chicken and vegetables and warm crusty bread was a treat to me after weeks of eating what I could get on the street. Even having to listen to the preaching didn't bother me too much, because I was kind of dozing with my high.

I found myself coming back often. Someone would pray and give a sermon, and there would generally be someone from the audience who would get up and tell something special that somebody called Jesus had done for him. They acted like this Jesus was still alive—and they looked so happy!

I heard many tell about how God had turned them around, guys who were not only outright dope fiends, but guys who all their lives had been bad hoodlums in the gutters of Harlem, the ghettos of Chicago, Philadelphia, and other rough places. They had been in the streets, just like me, and had grown up trying to beat the next man out of something with all kinds of schemes—con games, stealing, stickups, muggings, pimping— They told about the dirt in their lives and then they told what God had done for them, how He had cleaned them up and set them straight.

Sitting back in the audience, I couldn't really believe that everything they said was true, because I didn't know the guys when they were hooked. I just knew them now, when they looked okay.

But one day a man named Tony got up to talk, and he talked right to me. We had grown up together. I knew his whole family. Tony and I had hustled together, and I had bought my first dope from his sister Ollie.

"I was on the streets like some of you," he said, "so low I couldn't git no lower down."

I knew that was true. Tony'd gone all the way to being an addict ahead of me. But he always kept his appearance up because he stuck to stealing from cars. He was about the best short cracker around. That was a good fast way to make bread.

"Every time I turned around, I got busted," Tony

went on; "an' I had the withdrawals so bad in jail I thought I would die—" All the heads around me nodded in sympathy. They'd been there too; they knew how it was. "An' when I got out a couple of times, the OD's like to of kilt me. Lotsa times I got ahold of no-good dope that made me sick—"

Hard anger welled up inside me. *The nerve of those creeps burnin' him, sellin' him a lemon!*

Tony saw me watching him, listening intently to his story.

"Why, Bunky back there," he said, pointing right at me, "why, Bunky and I kept the jail doors hot, swingin' us in and out. If he wasn't already there when I got hauled in, he'd be comin' in shortly. I could count on that. Always, fer both us, dope and stealin', stealin' and dope. We wuz hooked anyway you looked at us. Floyd knows how it wuz with me—'bout like it is with you now, ain't that right, Bunky?"

I could feel every eye in the place turning to me. Even my high couldn't keep me comfortable when he was pointing to me like that, as a bad example. He looked so good up there—healthy and clean and high—the kind of high where it didn't seem like he'd ever come down. Maybe he'd found something that would last a little longer . . .

"Yeah, I wuz in bad shape," he said, "only then I come to find out what wuz wrong with me—and what I needed to git me straightened out." He was grinning at us like it was some kind of a happy joke he was going to tell. "I got sent off to this place they call Teen

Challenge, and they learned me about Jesus there. And, man, that Jesus is the answer to ever'thing!

"God sent Him to die fer me—an' you—so we wouldn't hafta suffer no more—so we could be free. He made it so I could kick my habit fer good and just be high, happy high, bein' with Him all the time. What wuz wrong with me wuz that I didn't know Jesus—and when I met Him, all my old life wuz gone."

When Tony sat down, some of the crowd clapped their hands a little. But I just sat there, thinking. I could tell Tony had turned around all right. I could tell that just by looking at him, seeing him all right-side-out and happy to be alive. It got to me.

I found myself thinking that Jesus must be real, 'cause Tony loved dope, and he shot it every time he could git his hands on it. Just as fast as he got out of jail, he got back to the needle. And he worked every kind of trickeration to support his habit—

I nudged Phil who had nodded off in the seat beside me, and he opened his eyes to stare.

"Reckon we could get to know Him too—this Jesus fellow?" I asked.

Phil blinked, like he was trying to understand, and grunted at me before his head toppled over to his shoulder and his soft snores started up again.

I thought about Tony a lot, but I still didn't understand exactly what had happened to him. What was it with this Jesus?

I got to where I went to soul-saving regular and got to know some of the other guys around. I wanted to find out more about how they got straight, and see if it could happen to me.

The folks that worked there, looked like they couldn't do enough for you. They'd give you individual counseling, put you on welfare if you needed it, send you to a detoxification hospital if you wanted to go—they'd help you with any problem you had, or thought you had.

This really bugged me. I couldn't understand how these people—squares—could remain on the up and up listening to the lies and tales that we told them day after day, and still keep on telling us that they loved us and that God wanted to accept us just like we were. We sure couldn't accept ourselves that way. And the world didn't accept us either.

But the people at the soul-saving station looked at us, every day, with a smile that loved clean through us. There was the Rev. they called Brother Richards and another Rev. named Brother Val. I didn't understand the "Brother" business. They didn't have the same last names, even, but everybody called them Brother. They even called me Brother. At first it felt funny to hear them say that, but pretty soon I was calling them "Brother" too—though it still didn't sound right to me.

And there were other things I didn't understand. I knew they had kids of their own. It didn't make sense to me how they could care what happened to us. They didn't owe us anything. And they weren't born angels—some of them had been addicts themselves. Some were only youngsters, in their late twenties or early thirties. But they had been able to pull out and get their lives straightened out from the gutters. Brother Tate was one, a young ex-addict who helped us all he could. And Brother Butler was another one.

I couldn't level with them. I kept telling them lies about myself because I wanted them to like me, and I didn't see how they *could* like me if they knew how I really was inside.

One day I felt so guilty about deceiving them that I could hardly stand it. I wanted to do right. But I couldn't admit what I really was, and it seemed like I couldn't get rid of my bad self until I admitted what was behind the false front I was always putting up. Tears that wouldn't stop rolled down my cheeks when the pastor preached a sermon and prayed over me. There was a hard lump in the middle of my chest that wouldn't swallow down. The back of my neck ached, and my shoulders were tied in knots.

Brother Richards and the pastor saw what was happening inside me and they quit praying and just started saying, "Praise the Lord." When they did that, something happened to the lump in my chest, and my shoulders and neck sort of relaxed, like I knew I was going to be all right pretty soon, like something big was going to happen in my life.

That scared me so bad I stayed away from the soul-saving station for a while. But after about three weeks, my stomach started tying itself in knots again, my highs didn't stay with me, and I knew I had to go back, no matter what it cost me. When I got to the front steps, I nearly tripped over a spotted pup, a dirty, skinny mutt lying at the foot of the steps, opening his eyes to look at me and batting his tail against the sidewalk but not making any move to leave, like he trusted me not to step on him, not to hurt him. Looking at him, I felt like maybe, finally, I was ready to trust somebody, too.

"Where you been, Brother Floyd?" Brother Richards asked me when I got inside.

"Yeah, Curly, we've missed you," Brother Val chimed in, slapping me on the back.

"Oh, Brother Val," I confessed, "I just got sick of myself comin' here and leadin' you on and seein' others do the same thing. I just couldn't take it, and so I had to pull away." Something in me wanted to surrender right then, but something else kept tugging at me. I stayed inside a few minutes, feeling guiltier and guiltier, and it got so bad I couldn't swallow. I slipped away when Brother Val went to answer the telephone and Brother Richards had to talk to somebody in his office.

That very day I got busted—in a shooting gallery—with six other guys. When the officers broke the door down I had a spike in my arm.

"Put that down!" the man yelled, looking straight at me.

"I'll put it down in a minute," I answered him. And I pushed the plunger to send myself to heaven just one more time. A dope fiend *couldn't* stop giving himself a shot when he was that close to it.

I've seen guys on the roof when the man came down on them yelling, "Hold it—or I'll shoot!" They didn't stop even then, but answered back, "*You* hold it, till *I* shoot," and they finished their shot, no matter what.

I knew they had me dead to rights that day. So I figured I'd take the rap and act like I owned the shooting gallery even though it really wasn't mine. But when I learned that they were going to try to put me away for three years, I fought the charge.

I wanted to find an out, like a rat looking for even the tiniest little hole to go through. I remembered what Tony had said at the soul-saving station about Teen Challenge, and while I was in the bullpen in jail, a youngster came through and heard me talking to somebody about it.

"Hey, man," he interrupted, "I was there once, at that Teen Challenge place. And I'd love to go back again. It was a swingin' program—I did six months with them." He had completed the program but gone back on the street afterward. I listened to him tell how they sent him out to a beautiful place in the mountains where a guy could lose himself and really think. They even had trades to teach you and help you find a good place in the world. It sounded perfect to me.

"How come you in here, then," I asked him. "How come you cut it loose when it was so good to you?"

"Aw, man," he said, looking real shook up about it,

"I should have stayed with the Lord, but I turned away. But I'm gonna talk to the judge and see can I try Teen Challenge again." He brightened up just talking about it, and I decided maybe it had some hope for me too.

I got in contact with the pastor down at the soul-saving station and asked him to tell me more about Teen Challenge. He sent me a lot of pamphlets. One of them was called, *A Positive Cure,* and it told what would happen if I went to Teen Challenge. He also sent me a "letter of recognition" to show the judge when I came up for trial, explaining that there was a place for me in Teen Challenge when I came out.

It took a month for me to get out of jail although the bail wasn't but a thousand dollars. I went to court two or three times asking for a reduction in my bail, but the DA refused to grant it. He didn't trust me out under bail, he said.

Finally one day the judge had my record in front of him. He looked at me from time to time while he thumbed through so many yellow sheets about me it looked like a whole library in itself. Then he squinted at the DA over his glasses and said, "Why don't you trust him? You know he'll come back. Why, he doesn't do anything *but* come back. One way or another you can't lose him. Let him out on bail and he'll be back all right. He can't help himself. Even if he doesn't come back willingly, he'll be back."

Everybody in the courtroom howled with laughter,

and the judge banged his gavel on the bench to get them to quiet down.

The DA was still unwilling.

"No, your honor," he said. I knew it was his job to be hard on me.

"Well," the judge said, "I can certainly understand your position in this—but I think I can grant a reduction in his bail anyway, and I will." Then he looked at me again.

"Now, Mr. Miles," he boomed, sounding quite hard, "what's this about your wanting to go to Teen Challenge? I can't believe that's the place for you, and you thirty-nine years old."

"I think I could find myself there, your honor," I told him. And I went on to explain about the soul-saving station and some of the men there who had gone to Teen Challenge. I thought I had him talked into it. But he had something else in mind.

"Tell you what," he offered. "I can see that you want a chance, so I'm giving you six months' probation on the condition that you go to the federal hospital in Lexington, Kentucky, and let them see if they can straighten you out. I don't know about this Teen Challenge business—"

I gave a big sigh of relief. At least I wasn't going to prison.

He shook his finger at me then. "Now listen, Floyd, and listen well. I'm giving you a break—but it's the last time. If you don't go—"

"Oh, I'll go all right," I said.

"If you don't go," he began again, "and if you ever come back before me I'll give you all the law allows. I'll put you away for three years next time. You understand that?"

"Don't worry, your honor," I lied, knowing all of a sudden that I had no intention of going to the hospital in Lexington. I'd never heard of anyone staying clean after he'd been there. It would just be a waste of time for me.

I managed to stay on the street for about three months before I was picked up again, for violation of my parole in not going to Kentucky. But I faced a different judge this time. He gave me just the six months I would have received from the charge in the first place, since I hadn't been caught in any more trouble. And he gave me a chance to go to Teen Challenge.

This time I knew I *had* to go someplace. Brother Richards gave me the fifteen cents I needed for carfare to Teen Challenge—one way. I looked at it in my hand for a minute.

"Where's the rest of the money, Brother Richards?" I asked him. "Where's my fifteen cents for coming back if they don't take me?" I knew there was always a waiting list. And I didn't want to be caught stealing anything down in Brooklyn—not even fifteen cents so I could get back to Harlem. There was a judge there, Judge Leibowitz. I didn't want to come before him if there was any way I could keep from it. He had a reputation for conducting a fair trial, but if you were found guilty, he'd throw it to you. Instead of handing out maybe thirty days for petty larceny like we were used to getting in other parts of the city, he'd sentence you to the maximum three years every time. I didn't want to get messed up with him!

"You go on down there," Brother Richards laughed, shoving playfully at me. "You ain't coming back—not for a while."

He made it sound kind of final.

Chapter IX

On Monday morning, I walked into the front door of Teen Challenge and met Brother Randy in the lobby. He welcomed me warmly, shaking my hand and patting my back like he had been spending his entire life just waiting for me to come in. We went to an office and right away he started asking me questions so he could fill in the blanks of a form he had on the desk in front of him.

When he asked my religion I thought about how many times I had cursed God. I had cursed Him for even living—if there was a God. I had cursed Him for making me black, for letting my wife die, cursed Him for every unhappy thing in my life, even the things I knew I had brought on myself. All this crossed my mind.

"You name it," I heard myself say. "Take yer pick and put it down—that's my religion." Randy burst out laughing—only it sounded like he was laughing on account of something happy inside him, not laughing at me.

"Praise the Lord," he said then. That's what everybody had said at the soul-saving station too, and I was puzzled. I didn't understand what there was to praise anybody for—

"It's all right, Floyd," Brother Randy said. "It's all right. You'll find out about God—sooner than you think." And then he chuckled to himself and accepted me into Teen Challenge that very day. I wondered what he was laughing about, and I didn't understand how I could be accepted so fast.

"Are you sure you mean *today*?" I asked. "Isn't there usually a waiting period—or something?"

"Usually," he admitted, rubbing his hand through his sandy brown hair, "but not for you. You're a special case—you see, we've been praying for you." He cackled out loud again, as if he was tickled to death at my being there. "Brother Floyd, you just don't have a chance, you don't have a chance."

I wasn't sure that I liked for things to move all that fast. But Brother Randy just kept chuckling to himself and muttering something about "Praise the Lord, Hallelujah!" and he sent me down to the dormitory at 416.

On my way out, I met a bunch of fellows in the lobby. They tried to encourage me, telling what they were doing in Teen Challenge and what God had done for them. Looking at those youngsters, I couldn't really believe that they had ever been in the same kind of fix I was in myself.

In the dormitory I felt stranger still, more out of place than ever. There were ten kids living where I was assigned and most of them were Puerto Ricans. They kept talking to each other in Spanish. I couldn't understand them. That made me even more uneasy, because I was afraid they were talking about me.

That night all of them went down to the prayer room, and I had to go along. It was part of the program. They were all shouting "Hallelujah!" and "Praise the Lord!" I kept quiet mostly, taking it all in. I'd never seen so many people walking around with Bibles before in my life.

"Are you staying with us, Brother?" someone asked me. I nodded, and he whacked me on the back. "Well, Praise the Lord, Brother, and God bless you." Then he gave me a great big bear hug.

That got me to wondering what kind of a place I'd gotten myself into. I sat down in the chapel when the others did, so as not to stick out like a sore thumb. In some ways it seemed like a nice enough place, but I was the oldest one there, and these kids kept hollering "Hallelujah!" I didn't know what it was all about.

Watching the guys in the dormitory, I had seen that there were some of them who weren't for real, who kept trying to sneak smokes—and one had a can of beer. I knew that was against the rules. *I better git the hell out of this place,* I said to myself. *It ain't fer me.*

But before I could sneak out, I ran into a fellow named Speedy, an old-timer like myself. He was on desk duty and saw that I was having some problems. He invited me to sit down beside his desk.

"The Lord really turned my life around," he said. I knew he'd been a pusher and a thief and all the rest of it, because we'd been in jail together, lots of times. Every bad thing he confessed, I knew it was true. He felt good, he said, and he looked beautiful to me.

"Floyd, you just hang on, brother," he said. "I guarantee that life's gonna change fer you." He held out his arms and showed me the black tracks up and down them, and the scars and dented-in places where they'd gotten infected from the spike. It was like he was trying to remind me that he'd been there too. His arms looked almost worse than mine. He'd been there, all right.

I promised him I'd stay on, for a day or two anyhow. And then something began to get to me. When I tried to pray, and when the youngsters got up to talk in chapel, and when I heard the beautiful sermons, suddenly my eyes were like faucets that wouldn't turn off. The tears just kept on running and running. I felt the heaviness of the bad things in my life.

And when Dave Wilkerson's uncle, Brother John, came, it seemed like he was talking right to me.

I was willing to give myself to the God he talked

about, to belong to Him, if He'd have me, and I wanted forgiveness all right.

It would be good to let this Jesus, God's Son, take away everything I'd ever done wrong. The preacher made it sound like He would, if I'd just give it all to Him. And so I walked up to the altar rail and got on my knees between two other guys who got there first.

I prayed out loud since everyone else seemed to be doing it, and said, "God, here I am. You can have me if You want me. I think I want to belong to You, God. And please forgive all my sins. I'm sorry I done 'em." And then I said, "In Jesus' name, Amen," because that's how the preacher had been ending his prayers.

When I said that name Jesus, I felt a hundred pounds lighter. Because everything I was guilty about, all the dirt I'd done to other people—everything I'd ever stolen, all the lies I'd ever told—all of a sudden they were gone, clean gone, like a whole bunch of bad things had gone out of me. I knew what they meant then about being saved. I was saved from all my badness. It was just as if it had never happened! And I didn't feel like I was going to have to shape up and change my life. Jesus was changing it for me, right then and there, making me clean from the inside out, just because He loved me so much and wanted me to keep Him company! It was like we had belonged together from the beginning of the world.

While I was still kneeling there, thanking Him for saving me, I felt Brother John ease in behind me and put his hands on my shoulders.

"Son," he said, "you need the Holy Spirit now that Jesus has saved you—to keep you strong to walk in your new life. Wouldn't you like to have the Holy Spirit?" he asked. "Wouldn't you like Jesus to baptize you in His Holy Spirit?"

I felt so wonderful, I didn't really think I needed anything else, but if Brother John thought I ought to have the Holy Spirit—whatever that was—and if Jesus wanted to give it to me, then I was all for it.

"Yeah!" I said. "I want *everything* Jesus wants to give me."

I started to pray like I heard the others praying. "Touch me with Your Spirit, Lord." Tears were running down my cheeks, but I didn't seem to be crying exactly. I was trying hard to receive the Spirit, but nothing was happening as far as I could tell.

I could hear some of the others guys who had received the Spirit, Jesus' Holy Spirit, inside themselves. They were praying with funny words I never heard before—"speaking in tongues," Brother John called it. I tried to imitate them, but it didn't work.

"Don't struggle so hard, Floyd," Brother John said. "Just talk to Jesus like you believe He's there, and ask Him to baptize you in His Holy Spirit. It's as simple as that. Because He's promised—"

I did what he said, not straining anymore, and WOW! Before I knew what was happening I was flat on the floor, crying, "Thank you, Jesus!" at the top of my lungs—because I knew He had done it. He had flooded me with His Holy Spirit, inside and outside! I knew that He belonged to me and I belonged to Him. And I saw that God was my real Daddy, and had been trying to tell me all along.

"Thank you, Jesus! Thank you, Jesus!" I shouted again. My shirt was wringing wet, like it had been drenched with the water gushing from a fire hydrant. And happy? I'd never been happier in my whole entire life!

And then I noticed that I was speaking in an unknown tongue myself. I wasn't trying to, but strangely beautiful words were flowing out of my mouth so fast I could hardly believe I was hearing myself. I didn't know what the words meant, but I knew that Jesus was real, and that He was with me forever. My life had turned all the way over. I was brand-new. I could feel the newness in me, almost like I had just been born.

After that night, I wanted to stay at Teen Challenge forever. They did let me complete their program and stay an extra month before they sent me to the mountains where they had another place, "God's Mountain," they called it, at Rehrersburg, Pennsylvania. They told me that I'd find even more blessings up there, but I couldn't believe it.

I hated to leave Brother Eisenberger. He was the first psychiatrist I ever came to know. I met him right after I was baptized in the Holy Spirit, and I saw the Lord in him the first time I looked at him. I let all my truth out to him. Always before, I had tried to hide things from the psychiatrists, to keep some secrets. But Brother Eisenberger didn't just ask me questions. He talked to me and gave me things to read about myself, things that told what he thought of me. He wasn't afraid to trust me with his feelings, and so I wasn't afraid to trust him with mine.

"God's Mountain" up at Rehrersburg was all they said it would be—and more. God had entered my heart in Brooklyn, and I took Him with me to the mountains. The first night there I was asked to testify, to tell what God had done for me. Everybody listened, and I didn't feel bashful or shy at all. In fact, it was hard for me to stop talking, because God had been so wonderful to me.

I wanted to stay at the farm forever, away from all the temptations and troubles of the world, but I knew my kids needed me. I had duties as a father since the Lord had restored me to health and strength in my mind.

Before leaving Pennsylvania, I had a chance to go to a lot of different churches and homes, witnessing all through the state. Best of all was an invitation to go to Lehigh Valley Prison and testify to youngsters there, telling how God could turn their lives around, like He had mine.

I wanted to go, all right, and tell them about how much Jesus loved them, but I was a little superstitious about it at first, kind of leery and shook up.

"Are you sure," I asked Brother Rook, who took me there, "are you sure that you checked it out with the warden and that I'm going to be allowed to come out the same day I'm going in?" It would be the first time I had ever gone into the front door of a prison and come out the front door the same day.

He laughed and looked me up and down.

"Brother Floyd," he said, "can't nobody lock you up now, never no more." And he went on to remind me of something I will never forget as long as I live:

"Remember, Brother Floyd, whom the Lord sets free is free indeed."

I nodded my head. The Lord had set me free by telling my heart I belong to Him and He belongs to me. And by letting me know that He is my real Daddy, my Heavenly Father—and all men are my brothers. I knew I didn't ever need to worry about any kind of prison ever again.

Epilogue

New blessings crowded into my life when I returned to Teen Challenge in New York as a Junior Staff Member. I was glad to be one of the black brothers because I had seen a lot of youngsters come in and leave in a hurry when they didn't see anyone who was black to talk to them, someone who had grown up in Harlem and understood what it was like to be there. Later, I went to work with addicts in Plainfield, New Jersey, trying to help them kick their habits.

Some addicts come in to see me after they heard I was a mainline heroin addict for nineteen years. They want to look at the black tracks on my arms to see if it's true. When they do, they think there's some hope for them, too.

"Whatcha usin'?" one boy asked me. "Methadone?" Methadone is a drug we use to help heroin users kick their habits and return to a useful place in society. It kind of takes the place of heroin for them, when they're not yet ready to go all the way with God and be free. Because the government provides it, they don't have to be hustling to support a habit anymore. They're not dangerous to other people like heroin addicts are. But they're still sick, and they know it when they have to depend on a drug to keep them able to function.

"No, I'm not using methadone," I told him. "I'm a Christian now. I'm using the Lord—and my faith in God. That's the only thing I'm on now—and I want to be on that the rest of my life."

He looked at me, stunned, and poked a finger at his long-haired companion—I couldn't be sure if it was a boy or a girl— "Get a load of what he says," he exclaimed. "What kinda bag is this guy comin' out of?"

I didn't argue with him, just tried to plant a seed so the Lord can provide a harvest later on when his highs bring him lower and lower until he hits the bottom and turns to the Lord.

Every day I pray for boldness, the Lord's boldness in me, so that I can speak out with wisdom to all who come to the clinic because they want to kick their habit. I want to tell them all that the Lord is the answer, the only answer.

Every time I go back to my old neighborhood, I

hear of somebody dying of an overdose, or getting stabbed or shot. Just seeing how the ones I left behind are still going down, their bodies falling apart, and their minds confused, breaks my heart. Because they don't have to be that way. I try to be real with them, to show them what God has done for me, and I pray and pray and pray and keep on praying to get them to come to the Lord.

Just the other day I ran into a fellow I hadn't seen for two or three years. We always called him Twenty Grand. He's still out there running the streets, with both of his hands swollen up like an elephant's leg.

"Man, I got it in quarters, pieces, however you want it," he said, thinking I was a good customer. I was surprised at how bad he looked.

"Man, ain't you tired?" I asked him, shaking my head. "How can you keep this up? Don'tcha know yer killin' yerself?"

He just laughed at me and wandered off after I tucked a piece of paper into his pocket, a tract explaining how Jesus can set him free. I pray that maybe he'll read it before he nods off after his next fix.

There are others I can't talk to at all, like the Lord is telling me, "Not now. It's not the right time yet." And so I just pray for them, and wait. One of them is Robert Scott, a good-looking boy who came in my office today. I pray for him too.

Somehow Robert Scott started me to thinking about the tests the psychologists had given me in prison, the tests where they had me draw a picture of a house, a tree, a woman, and a man and then asked me what I'd like to come back as, if I had another life to live on earth. Today my answer would be the same as it was then, during those nineteen years of hell, but for a different reason.

I didn't want to come back as anything then, because I was sick of the misery called life. I wouldn't want to come back as anything now, either—because I'd want to stay in heaven with Jesus. That's where I belong.

But mostly I don't think that far into the future. I just live as God gives me life from day to day. And I don't think of myself as an ex-addict, an ex-prisoner, and ex-tubercular, an ex-anything. I'm just Floyd Alexander Miles, who has been born again, and this time God is taking me all along the way, a completely new way.

It has been a way filled with miracles. I stop and think about it when I wake up in our clean, comfortable apartment, my new wife sleeping quietly beside me, our little son stirring in his pretty brown crib. And I pinch myself sometimes, just to be sure I'm not dreaming.

God has been so good to me it's hard to believe it. I have such a wonderful home, perfect health, and a good job with work that is meaningful to me, work where I can serve the Lord, pointing the ones lost in darkness to His light. God has given me a loving wife and a brand-new baby son. My teenage daughter lives with us, and she and my firstborn son, who lives with his grandmother and visits us on weekends, are growing in wisdom and understanding every day.

Oh, there are little differences of opinion among us, sometimes, things the Lord has to work out for us. But He is able.

"Look at what I was once," I tell my wife. "God's brought us so far already—He'll keep on bringing us along."

We sigh together, and she leans her head on my shoulder. It is so good to trust God to work everything out, even though we don't know just how He's going to do it. We can trust Him without knowing.

And sometimes, things go so smoothly that I almost get scared, like I'm expecting something bad to happen and spoil it all. Only then I remember to pray and put it all back in the hands of the Lord who made us. Then I can stop worrying.

My arms are still lined with long black tracks. But now the tracks are abandoned; nothing runs there anymore. I don't need tracks to run away on or to look for a place to belong. My Heavenly Father is with me wherever I go. I don't need tracks to follow Him. He lights the way.